J E780

WITHDRAWN

D1256412

Charles Lindbergh

CHARLES LINDBERGH

by Blythe Randolph

Franklin Watts
New York ∼ London ∼ Toronto ∼ Sydney ∼ 1990

Maps by Joe LeMonnier

Photographs courtesy of Library of Congress: pp. 2,; The Bettmann
Archive: pp. 26, 37, 91 (bottom), 119, 144; Brown Brothers: pp. 17,
49, 67, 73; Minnesota Historical Society: pp. 23, 33; Culver Pictures:
pp. 30, 43, 61, 63, 83 (inset), 115; UPI/Bettmann Newsphotos: pp.
45, 69, 79, 83, 90, 91 (top), 105, 124; AP/Wide World: pp. 109, 150.

Library of Congress Cataloging-in-Publication Data
Randolph, Blythe.
Charles Lindbergh / by Blythe Randolph.
p.   cm. —
Includes bibliographical references.
Summary: Presents a biography of Charles Lindbergh, from his early
years as an aviator to his controversial later life.
ISBN 0-531-15150-6.
ISBN 0-531-10918-6 (lib. bdg.)
1. Lindbergh, Charles A. (Charles Augustus), 1902–1974—Juvenile
literature.   2. Air pilots—United States—Biography—Juvenile
literature. [1. Lindbergh, Charles A. (Charles Augustus),
1902–1974.   2. Air pilots.] I. Title.
TL540.L5R26   1990
629.13'092—dc20
[B]   [92]   89-39713   CIP   AC

Contents

Charles Lindbergh

*To the memory
of my father*

"How Come He Never Got Famous?"

In 1957 a new film was released by Warner Brothers Studios called *The Spirit of St. Louis*. It was about the historic 1927 flight of Charles A. Lindbergh from New York to Paris. Lindbergh wrote the book between 1938 and 1953, and it was published in 1953 to wide acclaim. It was a Book-of-the-Month Club main selection and won the Pulitzer Prize for biography that year. Warner Brothers paid $1 million for the rights to make the film, an awesome sum at that time, and they hired the renowned actor James Stewart, who was both a box-office draw and a Lindbergh look-alike, to portray the young flier. Warner Brothers then engaged in a huge publicity campaign to market the film, fully expecting a huge hit.

Unfortunately, when the film was released, the expected crowds didn't show. People in Lindbergh's generation had had enough of the flier; he had been an active participant in the struggle to keep the United States out of World War II, and many people felt that he had been a traitor to his country. Even those who did not believe him disloyal felt that he had let the United States down at a crucial time.

Young people, on the other hand, who did not remember his position on World War II, simply didn't know who he was or what the fuss was about. The newsreels that they had seen showing fliers from World War II in combat made Lindbergh's flight seem dull in comparison. A cartoon in the magazine *The New Yorker* summed up their feelings. It showed a young boy leaving the movie theater with his father and saying, "If everyone thought what he did was so marvelous, how come he never got famous?"

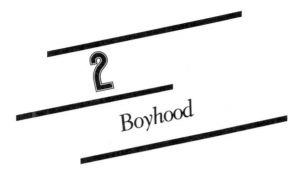

Boyhood

He was known for both courage and for ingenuity, and both qualities were certainly part of his ancestral background.

Lindbergh's grandfather was a Swedish peasant who was known—and revered—for both his physical and moral strength. His name was originally Ola Manson (or Mansson), and he had risen, despite his own father's death when the boy was five, to become a prominent landowner and a member of the Swedish parliament. Known as a fiery liberal, he fought for many social reforms, including outlawing the whipping post as a means of punishment and corporal punishment of servants by their masters, improvements in public transportation, and extension of suffrage. He was also a good friend and secretary to the crown prince of Sweden, who later became King Charles XV. His efforts at reform, however, enraged many of the nobility, who managed to have him charged with embezzlement. He was probably innocent, but the charge damaged his reputation, and he left for America in 1860 at the age of fifty, with a new wife of twenty (his first wife had died) and a newborn son, Charles Augustus, named for the new king. He also changed his own name to August Lindbergh.

Like many other Scandinavians before him, Lindbergh went to Minnesota, whose green forests reminded him of his native land. There he homesteaded a small piece of forestland near Sauk Center. Life, which was always difficult, became even more so two years after his arrival, when he suffered the loss of an arm in an accident. He survived—no mean feat in those days for a man over fifty—and learned to do as much work with one arm as most people do with two. Part of this was due to the fact that he was as technologically clever as his grandson would later be. For example, he devised a belt to which he could attach farming tools, some of which he had specially built.

Lindbergh's grandmother, the former Louise Carline, showed great bravery during these hard times despite her youth. During the Sioux uprising of 1862, the Lindberghs had to flee for their lives to a fort in nearby St. Cloud. During their rough encampment there, she gave birth to a daughter. Despite the fear of Indians that this experience left in her, on a later occasion when local Indians stole a specially designed axe that her husband needed, she followed them, demanded the return of the axe, and got it.

The Lindberghs' self-sufficient ways had an indelible influence on their son. From an early age Charles was expected to share in the many chores of their life. He was a dead shot with a gun and was expected to keep his family supplied with wild game. Ammunition was expensive, and he had to account for every spent cartridge. He became so proficient that if he missed one shot, he lined up two birds with the next so as not to waste ammunition. He was less successful at the local school that his father had helped to establish. Anxious to be in the woods, he had the worst attendance record at the school.

Despite his dislike of structured learning, young Charles was an avid reader. He also had a good example of learning in his father and was in addition influenced by his father's liberal leanings. He decided to become a lawyer, which necessitated his going to school. When he was twenty-one, he entered a private parochial school run by a priest. He paid his way by hunting and trapping and walked 10 miles (16 km) to school each day. He finished the course of study in one year and then entered law school at the University of Michigan. After receiving his law degree and clerking for one year in St. Cloud, he moved to Little Falls, Minnesota, a small town on the banks of the Mississippi. Boarding with a local family named La Fond, he fell in love their daughter, Mary. They married and had three children, two of whom survived infancy. He built a prosperous law practice by relying on two rules: charge low fees and never take a case unless you think your client is in the right. He invested his earnings in farmland, which in twenty years was worth about a quarter of a million dollars. Unfortunately, he lost his wife after only eight years of marriage. He left his children with his mother and went back to live in Little Falls, where he met Evangeline Land two years later.

Evangeline Lodge Land was the daughter of C. H. Land, a prominent Detroit dentist. Dr. Land, a Canadian whose ancestors included the founder of Hamilton, Ontario, not only built a large practice in his adopted city but was also well known as the inventor of porcelain crowns, high-temperature gas and oil burners and furnaces, and many smaller household devices. His wife's family were descendants of General Winfield Scott, hero of the Mexican War and presidential candidate, and both her father and her brothers were doctors. Evangeline Land, deeply interested in science herself, had received a Bachelor of Science degree from the University of Michigan at Ann Arbor, as well as a Master's Degree in science from Columbia University. She had gone to Minnesota to teach at the local high school. Part of her interest in Charles seemed to stem from her current dislike of her position. Little Falls had not proved to be the exciting western town that she had imagined, and her proud ways had landed her in trouble several times with the high school principal. Finally, she quit her job, and she and Charles were married on March 27, 1901. After a honeymoon in San Francisco, they began to build a home on 110 acres which Charles had bought several years earlier, 2 miles (3.2 km) outside Little Falls. However, when Evangeline found out that she was pregnant, she decided to return home for the birth. Charles Augustus Lindbergh, Jr., was born in Detroit on February 4, 1902, and was delivered by his great-uncle. When Evangeline and Charles, Jr., returned to Little Falls, their new home—a handsome three-story house— was ready. Unfortunately, this residence burned down when Charles was three years old, and a simpler home was built in its place.

There was now less need for a large home, because Charles and Evangeline's marriage was in difficulties. It had not been successful almost from the beginning, and their main reason for staying together was the birth of their son. The question of divorce never really arose, however, because Charles Lindbergh, Sr., was going into politics, and in the largely Roman Catholic community, a divorce would ruin him politically and socially. When he was elected the Republican congressman from Minnesota's Sixth District in 1907, he and Evangeline decided to stay together for appearance sake, but spend some time apart from each other. This meant that less time each year would be spent in Little Falls. In September of each year Charles and his mother would travel to Washington, D.C., to be with Charles, Sr., stopping on the way for two weeks in Detroit with her family. They would spend some months in the capital and then, after stopping in Detroit for another visit, would be in Little Falls in the late spring and summer months.

~

The young Charles was a self-sufficient little boy, regardless of the inner turmoil that his parents' separation caused him (he was never to refer to it in his memoirs). He adored both his parents and loved being able to be with both of them in Washington, despite Charles, Sr.'s, dedicated attitude toward his governmental responsibilities (he rose at 4 A.M. and was at work by 5). The visits with his father, however, were the only things that Charles liked about Washington. He much preferred the outdoor life of Minnesota, and from an early age he was an avid outdoorsman. From the age of six he had his own gun and soon became an expert marksman. He was forever wandering through the neighboring woods, collecting specimens and studying woodcraft. He tamed a chipmunk, swam and fished in the creek, built himself a raft and a garden hut, and spent hours sitting beside the Mississippi.

Charles was also responsible for a number of household chores, including filling the icebox with ice, and when he was nine years old he developed and constructed a system for moving the ice from the icehouse, which was a short distance from the house, to the icebox. Years later he would write about it in an article for the Minnesota Historical Society (reprinted in Leonard Mosley's biography of Lindbergh, p. 11):

Of course these cakes [of ice] were always surrounded by sawdust to keep them from melting during the hot summer months. I would shovel the sawdust off a cake, split it carefully into smaller chunks of a size that would just fit into our icebox, and then with a pair of tongs drag one of the chunks up on top of the sawdust. Since it was too heavy for me to lift up out of the icehouse onto the ground, I had constructed a slide from 2-by-6-inch planks. With a rope attached to the tongs, it was not difficult for me to pull the ice chunks up the slide. Then I would tip my express cart over on its side, push the ice chunk up against it, and tip the cart upright again. I would pull the cart to a stake in the ground well in front of the kitchen steps, to which I had fastened one end of a heavy wire. The other end of the wire I had attached to a ring screw embedded in the house well above the kitchen porch. I would hook the ice tongs to a pulley that ran over this wire and then haul the pulley, slide the ice chunk over the floors and into the pantry where we kept the icebox against the north wall. There I had another slide, also made of planks, to get the ice into its compartment.

This early interest in technology was enhanced by the time Charles spent in Detroit, where he was allowed to conduct scientific experiments in his grandfather's lab-

*Young Lindbergh at eight years
of age, with his father*

oratory. His mother first enrolled him in school in Washington when he was eight, but he was not an attentive pupil. He would attend eleven schools within a ten-year period but would never finish a full academic year in any of them. This was partly because his family moved around so much but also because he just never learned to enjoy sitting in a classroom.

When Charles was ten years old, his father arrived from Washington one summer behind the wheel of a Model T Ford, which he had bought for Mrs. Lindbergh. Charles's legs were still too short to reach the pedals of the car, and for some months he suffered as he watched his parents—neither of whom was mechanically minded—deal badly with the driving and maintenance of the car. As soon as he was tall enough to reach the pedals, he quickly became a better driver than either of them and drove his mother all over the area. When his father sought reelection in 1913, Charles, Jr., acted as chauffeur so that his father could campaign all over the district.

This campaign was particularly important to Charles, Sr. He felt very strongly about certain national issues. Unlike many of his constituents, Charles, Sr., was extremely liberal—some even said he was a socialist. He was very critical of the big financial powers of the day, such as the Rockefellers and the Morgans, and even wrote a book, *Banking and Currency and the Money Trust*, which condemned many common Wall Street practices. He was also a pacifist and opposed U.S. involvement in the conflict in Mexico in which President Wilson was trying to intervene, as well as U.S. intervention at the beginning of World War I. However, like most of the farmers he represented, he favored the same market protections that they favored, and he was returned to Congress in 1913. Charles was happy for his father but later admitted that as much as he admired him, at the time he had rarely listened to the issues and was much more concerned with the workings of the automobile.

In the summer of 1915, Charles Lindbergh, Sr., was asked by Congress to lead a two-man expedition through the wilderness. The purpose of the trip was to seek the source of the Mississippi and write a report on its dam system, which was said to be in trouble. Charles, Sr., decided to take his son as the other person, and for six weeks the two fought sun, flies, and mosquitoes to accomplish the task. They stayed in lumberjack camps and with Indians, and Charles was made an honorary member of the Chippewa tribe. He also got better acquainted with his father, who talked to him about his political values, ambitions, and motivations. Charles never forgot this trip and felt that at the end of it he knew his father as an individual, not just as a parent.

~

In 1916 the elder Lindbergh sought the Republican nomination for senator. Unfortunately, he opposed America entering World War I and was also chosen to investigate charges that the Roman Catholic Church was preventing freedom of speech, thought, and conscience. In a largely Roman Catholic area such as Minnesota, this was political suicide, and he was roundly defeated. Two years later, when he tried to run for governor, the same two issues came back to haunt him, and he was defeated again. In effect, his political career was finished, although he would make two other attempts to win office.

Meanwhile, as soon as the campaign of 1916 was over, Evangeline and Charles, Jr., drove to California, a trip that, because of bad weather, took forty days. They took a cottage at Redondo Beach, and Charles was enrolled in the local high school. As usual, he was not a good student, preferring to teach himself and resenting the authority of others. As a result, he frequently played hooky and wandered the beach, collecting shells and daydreaming.

Then one day Evangeline learned that her mother was gravely ill with cancer and was not expected to recover. She and Charles, Jr., immediately left for the East and for the first time planned to spend the winter on the farm. America was now involved in World War I, and Charles, Sr., believed that they should try to make themselves self-sufficient on the farm in order to help the war effort. As a result, Charles, Jr., took over the complete management of the farm while Evangeline tended to her ailing mother, whom she had brought to Little Falls.

It was a big job for a fifteen-year-old boy, but Charles's only complaint was that it was virtually impossible to run a farm and go to school, too. In that regard, he had a bit of luck. The government announced that, because of food shortages, it was vital that farms produce as much as possible. As a result, any boy wishing to work full-time on his farm would be given full credit for the period he was away. Charles immediately left school and rose at 5 A.M. every day to deal with the numerous chores: feeding the animals, milking cows, building pigsties and a duck pond, buying new stock and farm machinery, and repairing the machinery. At night he slept on the screened porch, no matter how cold it was, and gazed at the sky and the stars. He thoroughly enjoyed farming and had no reason to think that farming wouldn't be his life. But with November 1918 and the end of the war, his life changed.

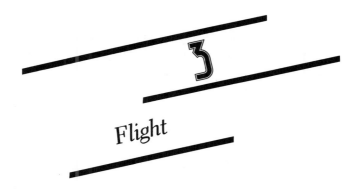

Flight

Before the war ended, Charles had wanted to enlist in the Army Air Corps and join the air fight in France, but he wasn't old enough. With the end of the war and the strong encouragement of his mother and father, he began to study college catalogs. He chose the University of Wisconsin, "probably more because of its lakes than because of its high engineering standards," he was later to write. His mother went with him, having secured a science-teaching post in Madison, Wisconsin.

College, for Lindbergh, was not a success. As always, he found formal education stifling and resented having his assignments chosen by the professors. He also resented the rules and regulations of college life, which he felt that he did not need, and had little in common with his fellow students, who seemed only interested in having a good time. They were interested in drinking and smoking, and Lindbergh abstained from alcohol, cigarettes, coffee, and even cola drinks. They loved to dance, and Lindbergh never learned how. His fellow males were very interested in girls, and Lindbergh thought girls were silly, shameless, or both, and went home to be with his mother every night. In the three semesters he attended the university he never went out on a date. Years later he would confess to film star Lillian Gish that he had never seen one of her films, which were box office hits during his college years.

The one activity that he enjoyed in his spare time was motorbiking. He had bought a motorbike before leaving Little Falls and had terrified the local citizenry with his daredevil antics. His two closest friends in college were also motorbikers, and the three of them had a wild time racing through the woods beyond Lake Mendota. Charles was the most fearless and undertook any number of challenges and dares, always coming out relatively unscathed. Once, in trying to navigate a turn at the bottom of a steep hill, he crashed but almost immediately figured out what he did wrong and repeated the stunt, without injury.

Despite these adventures, he was still interested in learning how to fly and wrote to the Nebraska Aircraft Company, which advertised that it would give free flying instruction to anyone who bought one of their Lincoln Standard planes. He wrote them that although he could not afford to buy a plane, he was prepared to pay them to teach him how to fly. They agreed to do so for $500, and in March 1922 he left Madison and university life after three semesters and took off on his motorbike for Lincoln. His mother returned to Detroit, where she would live for the rest of her life.

Lindbergh made his first airplane flight on April 9, 1922, and knew that he had found his life's calling. He

Lindbergh driving his motorbike in June 1921

was later to write in his book *The Spirit of St. Louis* (pp. 246–47):

Science, freedom, beauty, adventure: what more could you ask of life? Aviation combined all the elements I loved. There was science in each curve of an airfoil, in each angle between strut and wire, in the gap of a spark plug or the color of the exhaust flame. There was freedom in the unlimited horizon on the open fields where one landed. A pilot was surrounded by beauty of earth and sky. He brushed treetops with the birds, leapt valleys and rivers, explored the cloud canyons he had gazed at as a child. Adventure lay in each puff of wind. I began to feel that I lived on a higher plane than the skeptics of the ground; one that was richer because of its very association with the element of danger they dreaded, because it was freer of the earth to which they were bound. In flying, I tasted a wine of the gods of which they could know nothing. Who valued life more highly, the aviators who spent it on the art they loved, or these misers who doled it out like pennies through their antlike days? I decided that if I could fly for ten years before I was killed in a crash, it would be a worthwhile trade for an ordinary lifetime.

Unfortunately, Lindbergh had been assigned an unreliable instructor who found any excuse not to show up. On those days he didn't, Lindbergh spent the time waiting for him by learning about airplanes from mechanics working at the airfield. He was resentful, however, about not spending as much time in the air as possible. He was further discouraged by the news that the company's training plane was about to be sold to a barnstorming pilot named Erold Bahl, but this turned out to be a blessing. When Bahl turned up, and Lindbergh saw his skill with the plane, he knew that he had to learn everything Bahl had to teach him. As Leonard Mosley tells it in his book *Lindbergh: A Biography* (pp. 36–37):

Lindbergh approached him and hesitantly asked him whether he could tag along as a helper during Bahl's forthcoming tour.

The older man shook his head. "I don't need any help where I'm going—county fairs, town fetes, that sort of thing," he said. "There's always someone around to help you push the plane."

Lindbergh took a deep breath. "It won't cost you anything. I'll pay my own expenses."

Again Bahl shook his head. And then something about the look of this callow youth, the air of quiet desperation that seemed to hang around him, touched his sensibilities.

"What's your name, son?"

"I'm Slim Lindbergh. I've been learning to fly here, but now it looks as if they've run out of training planes. And trainers," he added bitterly.

Bahl said, "I guess it'll be all right for you to tag along. If you can look after yourself, that is."

A smile that would one day be famous broke across the young man's face.

"When do we leave!" he cried.

Barnstorming was the rage, and a good barnstormer could get $5 per person, a healthy sum in those days, for taking anyone interested up for a ride. For several weeks Lindbergh accompanied Bahl through Nebraska, Kansas, and Colorado, flying low over a community to raise interest and then selling tickets. Lindbergh started as mechanic and ticket seller and was so good at these tasks that Bahl decided to pay his expenses. Lindbergh then

~
25

*Wing-walking was a popular
barnstorming stunt.*

suggested that to drum up more trade in the next town, he himself would climb out on the wing of the plane and wave to the people on the ground. As challenging as this would be to anyone, it was even more challenging to Lindbergh at this time. Despite his bravery, he had a fear of falling from a great height and kept having nightmares about it. However, he taught himself how to wing-walk and did it for the remainder of the tour.

Back in Lincoln after the tour was over, Lindbergh met Charlie and Kathryn Hardin, who had come to give an exhibition of wing-walking, stunts, and parachuting. The impact of the latter on Lindbergh was enormous. He would later write in *The Spirit of St. Louis* (p. 240):

I watched him strap on his harness and helmet, climb into the cockpit and, minutes later, a black dot, fall off the wing two thousand feet above our field. At almost the same instant, a white streak behind him flowered out into the delicate, wavering muslin of a parachute—a few gossamer yards grasping onto air and suspending below them, with invisible threads, a human life, a man who by stitches, cloth, and cord, had made himself a god of the sky for this immortal moment.

He went to the Hardins and told them that he wanted not only to parachute but to double-jump. This meant that he would jump out of the plane, free-fall, open one parachute, float, cut himself loose from it, free-fall, open the second parachute, and float to the ground. Hardin made parachutes and sold them to fliers, and when Lindbergh assured him that he would buy one—after the jump—Hardin agreed to take him up. In packing the parachute for the jump, Hardin discovered that he was without the twine with which to fasten one parachute to the other for the double jump. So he tied the two together with package string. After Hardin and Lindbergh had climbed to 2,000 feet, Hardin gave Lindbergh the sign to jump. Lindbergh did, falling free until the first chute opened. He then cut away the first chute with his knife and began to free-fall again. The second chute refused to open as quickly as it should have but it finally did, and Charles landed unharmed. Interestingly, the incident seemed to end his fear of falling, and he was never plagued with it again. It was his proudest moment. He later wrote in *The Spirit of St. Louis*: "I'd stepped to the highest level of daring—a level above even that which airline pilots could attain. . . . I'd left my role of apprentice far behind."

Lindbergh also worked with the Hardins to learn stunts, such as how to hang by his teeth from a thin wire below the wing, how to land on marked targets, and how to do stand-up landings. He parlayed these techniques—plus his parachuting and mechanical abilities—into a job with a pilot named H. J. "Cupid" Lynch, and the two of them—plus Lynch's dog Booster—barnstormed all over Kansas, Nebraska, Wyoming, and Montana. Lindbergh acted as mechanic, parachutist, and wing-walker and even became adept at standing on the wing while Lynch put the plane into a loop. He was called "Daredevil Lindbergh" but insisted that his special foot straps and a belt around his waist, which was attached to cables on the wing pins, made the stunt much easier than it looked.

Soon after bad weather set in, Lindbergh went to spend the winter with his father in Minneapolis. While there, he convinced his father to sign the guarantee on a loan of $900 from his bank in Little Falls and took the money to Souther Field, Georgia, where the army was holding auctions of surplus equipment, including planes from World War I. There he found a creaky Curtiss Jenny with a tattered canvas, checked it carefully, and decided that the 90-horsepower engine was still good. It had a top speed of 70 miles per hour (113 kmph) and could fly no higher than 1,700 feet (518 m), but Lindbergh paid $500 for it and began his life as a barnstormer.

It suited him to perfection. He flew all over the Midwest as far west as Colorado and as far south as Texas. There was no space in the plane for a suitcase, so his personal baggage consisted of a toothbrush, a razor, and a cake of soap. His adventures during this period supplied him with anecdotes for years. Once, when flying in Texas, he was forced to put down on the main street of a small town called Uvalde. This he managed beautifully, but on takeoff, one of his wheels hit a rut in the street, and the plane's nose went into the local hardware store. Fortunately, the store's owner was so enthralled by the plane that he refused to let Lindbergh pay for the damage, saying that the moment was worth all of the broken glass.

At one point Evangeline Lindbergh joined him when he was flying nearby, and for ten days she threw overboard advertising leaflets, sold tickets, and learned flying techniques. She loved both flying and being with her son, and it was a special time for both of them.

In the summer of 1923, Lindbergh joined his father, as the latter was again seeking the nomination for the Senate. The elder Lindbergh went up in the plane with his son for the first time and was soon distributing campaign leaflets from the air. Later in his biography of Lindbergh, Leonard Mosley would write (p. 47):

Armed with a bundle of hundreds of sheets of campaign literature, Lindbergh [Sr.] climbed into the open-front cockpit of the "Jenny." As was customary in the early

biplanes, Charles, Jr., the pilot, took his place at the controls in the cockpit behind his father. By prearrangement, Lindbergh was to throw out the bills when his son rocked the plane and nodded. He did so when the signal was given, but instead of throwing the leaflets a few at a time, Lindbergh threw out the whole stack of literature at once and the bundle sharply hit the plane stabilizer. Fortunately, no damage was done, but as Charles, Jr., observed many years later, "the distribution of the literature in the town wasn't very broad." He recalled that "my father's face was quite serious when he looked back at me after the thud."

Unfortunately, an accident soon damaged the landing gear and the propeller, and Lindbergh's campaign help was at an end. It probably would have made no difference. His father was the underdog and did not get the nomination.

Meanwhile, Lindbergh had heard that Lambert Field, St. Louis, was holding the International Air Races, and he took off for Missouri. There he was exposed to more kinds of planes than he had ever seen before. In addition, he ran into a young man he had first met in Lincoln, Bud Gurney, who had coined Lindbergh's nickname "Slim." They planned to do some stunts together, as Bud was a parachute jumper. Unfortunately, on his first jump with Lindbergh, Bud broke his arm, which ended their plans. At loose ends, Lindbergh decided to sell his plane and go into the army as an air cadet.

Lindbergh with his mother,
Evangeline Land Lindbergh

~
31

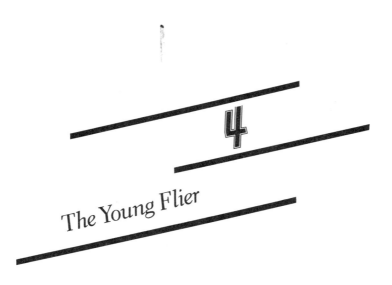

4

The Young Flier

Lindbergh's decision to join the army was the result of a conversation with a man named Marvin Northrup, who owned a small aircraft manufacturing company near St. Louis. They had met at the International Air Races, and Lindbergh had talked to Northrup about his desire to be an airline pilot. The problem, Lindbergh had said, was that it would probably be some time before commercial flying got going. What should he do in the meantime?

Northrup had suggested that he become an army air cadet and spend a year learning everything the army could teach him about planes—and get paid for it. On receiving his commission, he could either stay on in the army or go into the army reserve. When Lindbergh heard how much flying he would do, he immediately applied, and in March 1924, he reported to the army air base in Brooks Field, Texas.

This turned out to be a terrific decision for Lindbergh. The course was extremely difficult. Only 18 of the

Lindbergh as an air cadet in 1925

104 cadets stayed the entire year and received their second lieutenant commissions. But Lindbergh graduated at the top of his class. He even swallowed his dislike of studying, lectures, and examinations and came in first in both oral and written tests as well as actual flying. He was also able to learn all sorts of new flying techniques—formation flying, high-altitude maneuvers, strafing, bombing, gunnery, photography, and precision takeoffs and landings. Finally, he learned how to fly more powerful planes than he had previously flown, planes that could climb to over 12,000 feet (3,600 m). He was not the most popular cadet, but he was admired and respected, even if he was always too much of a "stick" to be really well liked. The only way that Lindbergh showed a sense of fun was through his love of practical jokes. He put itching powder in the pajamas of several cadets and a live snake in the bed of another cadet. One loud snorer found his bed on the roof of the bunkhouse one night, and once Lindbergh even let a skunk loose in a classroom.

One sad incident broke into this good time. Lindbergh's father, who was trying once more to get himself elected to office—this time as governor of Minnesota—fell ill early in the campaign and was taken to the Mayo Clinic in Rochester, Minnesota, where he was found to have an inoperable brain tumor. He died in May 1924, and Lindbergh, who had been allowed to visit his father before he died, was again given leave to go to the funeral in Minneapolis. Afterward, Lindbergh took his father's ashes in his plane and scattered them over his father's childhood town of Melrose, Minnesota.

Charles didn't have much time to mourn his father's death. The course was just too grueling. He did beautifully, but just ten days before it ended, an incident occurred that almost finished it—and him—when his plane interlocked with another cadet's, in the air, and both fliers quickly had to bail out.

After graduating, Lindbergh wrote to the government to ask for a commission in the army. While he was waiting for an answer, he resigned from active service, joined the army reserve, and headed for Lambert Field in St. Louis.

While there, he received a letter from a man named Wray Vaughan, who was president of the Mil-Hi Airways and Flying Circus in Boulder, Colorado. Vaughan offered Lindbergh a job at $400 per week, and Lindbergh accepted—not so much because of the money but because of the location. Charles had become interested in air currents and the resulting turbulence around canyons, glaciers, and mountain ranges. He thought that a job in the Rockies would give him a chance to study this phenomenon.

The "circus" consisted of a decrepit airplane in which he had barnstormed three years earlier. He was expected not only to take passengers on $5 rides every day but also to give a fireworks display every evening with Roman candles and streamers attached to the plane. This was a particularly dangerous mission because it involved flying in darkness with no airfields, the plane had to be landed in terrain that was sometimes rougher than it looked from the sky, takeoffs had to be made with only the headlights of a car as a guide, and landings had to be made without any light at all—except the blinding light from the Roman candles!

Before Lindbergh had been hired by the flying circus, he had met Bill and Frank Robertson at Lambert Field. These two men, who had been fliers in World War I, now owned their own small aircraft company and were trying to get the St. Louis/Chicago airmail route contract. While Lindbergh was working with the flying circus, they got the contract, and Charles headed back to Lambert Field. He chose two men to fly with him, two cadets who had been with him in Texas. They began flying in mid-April 1926 and through the summer flew mostly without incident. Moreover, 98 percent of their flights made the intended connection in Chicago. When bad weather set in during the fall, however, the situation changed. One day in September, the Chicago airport was blanketed by a high fog, and Lindbergh ran out of gas and was forced to parachute out of the plane. However, the plane nearly crashed into him. He later wrote in his book *We* (pp. 183–84):

Soon [the ship] came into sight, about a quarter of a mile away, and headed in the general direction of my para-chute. I put the flashlight in a pocket of my flying suit preparatory to slipping the parachute out of the way if necessary. The plane was making a left spiral of about a mile diameter, and passed approximately 300 yards away from my chute, leaving me on the outside of the circle. I was undecided as to whether the plane or I was descending the more rapidly and glided my chute away from the spiral path of the ship as rapidly as I could. The ship passed completely out of sight, but reappeared in a few seconds, its rate of descent being about the same as that of the parachute. I counted the five spirals, each one a little further away than the last, before reaching the top of the fog bank.

After Lindbergh landed in a cornfield, he found the plane in another cornfield 3 miles (4.8 km) away. The mailbags, luckily, had not broken, and Lindbergh immediately got them on a train for delivery.

*Delivering the mail by air was one of
the first commercial uses of airplanes.*

On another occasion two months later, Lindbergh was caught in a snowstorm and again ran out of gas while circling and trying to find a place to land. Once more, he was forced to parachute, this time into 70-mile-per-hour (112-kmph) winds at 13,000 feet (39,000 m). The wind made for a wild descent, but Lindbergh finally made it to the ground—on top of a barbed-wire fence! When the wrecked plane was found, the mail was still in good shape.

Despite these incidents, Lindbergh and his two fellow pilots continued to fly in all kinds of weather, even when other fliers refused to go up. They received little attention for their exploits, although Lindbergh set his first aviation record as the first American pilot to have made four emergency jumps from a plane.

During this time, Lindbergh was living a life that seemed to him to be almost too good to be true. He loved flying so much that, even on his days off, he flew passengers to locales around the Midwest and did exhibition stunt flying. His only problem at the time was the lack of a bigger challenge—a challenge that was about to appear on the horizon.

5
The Spirit of St. Louis

The seeds for this challenge were planted in 1919. A Frenchman living in the United States, Raymond Orteig, owner of the Brevoort and Lafayette hotels in New York, went to a dinner honoring Eddie Rickenbacker, the American flying ace of World War I. Rickenbacker had spoken of the great friendship that existed between the French and American peoples and said that he looked forward to the time when the two countries would be linked by aviation. Orteig, impressed, offered $25,000 (worth about five times that amount today) to any person or group that could fly from New York to Paris within the next five years.

No one took him up on this offer, because planes were simply not capable of making such a journey at that time. By 1926, however, when Orteig renewed his offer, technology had improved to the point that such a trip could at least be considered. Almost immediately, a famed French flier, Rene Fonck, appeared on the scene. Fonck had made a considerable reputation for himself during World War I as a flier, and as a result had extensive financial backing. He asked an aviation designer, Igor Sikorsky, to design for him a biplane with three engines and propellers, large enough to carry a crew of four. Unfortunately, the plane was far too weighted down with crew, fuel, and supplies (including four dozen American-made croissants for the French people) to become airborne. In trying to take off, it crashed, and its fuel supply ignited. Two of the four men aboard died.

Fonck's failure was taken as a challenge to Lindbergh. He believed that Fonck's major error was in trying to take so much weight—including crew—with him. He believed that a single-engine plane—carrying minimum equipment and one person, the pilot—would stand a better chance of making the journey. All the remaining weight could therefore be assigned for fuel. Charles decided that this was a challenge that he could not resist.

He began to approach St. Louis businessmen, promoting the trip as a civic tribute to St. Louis. It took several months to get enough people interested in the project, but finally he was able to raise $15,000 from such men as Albert Lambert—for whom Lambert Field was named—a part owner in one of the local newspapers, a local insurance broker, a local bank president, and his boss, Frank Robertson.

Lindbergh then began to approach aviation companies, but neither Fokker nor Wright-Bellanca was interested in selling him a single-engine plane for such a trip. They believed that no single-engine aircraft could possibly make it, and they did not wish to become involved in what they saw as a fruitless enterprise.

Lindbergh mailed out a number of requests to other companies, but none was interested except Ryan Aircraft, a small company in San Diego that was willing to work with Lindbergh for the designated amount.

Lindbergh was worried. No one had ever heard of Ryan, and the work would take several months. Meanwhile, other competitors were beginning to announce that they were soon going to try to make the trip. Lindbergh was afraid that one of them would succeed before he could get his plane built. He was about to give up, but his backers, who were now highly enthusiastic, convinced him to at least check out Ryan Aircraft. He flew to San Diego in February 1927, and one of the backers soon received the following telegram:

BELIEVE RYAN CAPABLE OF BUILDING PLANE WITH SUFFICIENT PERFORMANCE STOP COST COMPLETE WITH WHIRLWIND ENGINE AND STANDARD INSTRU-MENTS IS TEN THOUSAND FIVE HUNDRED EIGHTY DOLLARS STOP DELIVERY WITHIN SIXTY DAYS STOP RECOMMEND CLOSING DEAL—LINDBERGH

The backers wired back to close the deal.

Lindbergh recognized almost immediately how lucky he was to have found Ryan Aircraft. The group of highly dedicated men that made up the company were excited by this new challenge and put virtually all other work aside for the almost two months it took to design and build the aircraft. Lindbergh worked with them on every detail, sometimes for as long as eighteen hours a day. When the plane was finished, it was an odd-looking but very fast machine that Lindbergh was convinced would take him across the Atlantic.

While the plane was being built, Colonel Richard

E. Byrd and his crew, who were planning to fly the Atlantic in a tri-motored Fokker, crashed during a trial run. Damages to the plane and injuries to the crew were minimal, but it caused a scheduling delay. Meanwhile, two army competitors crashed and were killed on takeoff on the very day that Lindbergh's plane, which had been christened *Spirit of St. Louis*, was brought out of the factory. The whole company stood and watched while Lindbergh took the plane up for the first time (*The Spirit of St. Louis*, p. 112):

[It was] as though some child of theirs was going away to war. Their part was done. For them, the flight had started. For two months theirs had been the active part, while I stood by watching their craftsmanship. Now, the roles are reversed, and I'll have the field of action. Now, the success of their efforts depends upon my skill; and my life upon their thoroughness.

He was ready to go and waiting for the weather to clear over the Rocky Mountains when news came that two French fliers, Nungesser and Coli, had successfully taken off from Le Bourget Airport near Paris and were now making their way across the Atlantic toward New York. When Ryan's chief engineer and designer, Donald Hall, said that he hoped the two fliers didn't make it, Lindbergh angrily told him not to say that and began making preliminary plans to make a flight across the Pacific Ocean instead. Thirty-six hours later, however, it became clear that the two fliers had not, in fact, made it, and Lindbergh took off for Lambert Field, flying all night over the Rocky Mountains. He landed in St. Louis on May 11, 1927, and his backers came out to Lambert Field to greet him. They had planned an elaborate series

Lindbergh picks up his plane, the
Spirit of St. Louis, *in California*

of lunches, dinners, and celebrations, but Lindbergh convinced them that time was of the essence and that he should go on to New York immediately. When he arrived at Curtiss Field in Mineola, Long Island, the same day, he got his first taste of what it was like to be a celebrity. Hundreds of photographers and reporters were there, all asking what he considered to be ridiculous questions. He made the front page of the *New York Times* the next morning, and when he arrived back at Curtiss Field, he found even more journalists waiting for him. Several of his competitors also showed up, and Commander Byrd made the extremely generous offer to Lindbergh that he use the much longer runway at Roosevelt Field, which he had built.

However, the weather was not cooperating, and Lindbergh had to wait almost a week for it to clear over the Atlantic. Meanwhile, his mother, who was being driven crazy by reporters in Detroit, came to New York briefly to see her son. Lindbergh also visited Theodore Roosevelt's home in Oyster Bay, Long Island, met other aviators, and also met a man who would later become a good friend, the financier Harry Guggenheim. He was also assigned a publicity man, Dick Blythe, from Wright Aeronautical Corporation, the company that had made the engine for the *Spirit of St. Louis*.

On the night of May 19, 1927, Dick Blythe planned to take Lindbergh for an evening of fun and relaxation in New York, with accompanying publicity, but on the way to the theater they stopped to call Doc Kimball, their weatherman, who informed them that the weather was clearing over the Atlantic. All thoughts of a night on the town disappeared, as Lindbergh needed to get airborne as quickly as possible.

Lindbergh had one immediate problem. There was supposed to be a sixty-day waiting period between the

*Lindbergh's lifelong friend, financier
and millionaire Harry Guggenheim*

time the flier entered the Orteig competition and the takeoff. But if he waited that long, another competitor could easily take off and make it before he did. He called one of his backers, Harry Knight, of the *St. Louis Globe-Democrat*. What if he successfully completed the flight but was denied the money because of a technicality?

"To hell with the money," Knight replied. "When you're ready to take off, go ahead."

Lindbergh got some supper and tried to sleep. He knew that he had a long trip ahead of him. Unfortunately, a friend who didn't realize he was sleeping disturbed him, and he never was able to go back to sleep. He was up at 2:15 A.M. and down to the plane hangar at 3, still worried that one of his competitors was going to take off before him, but everyone else was still too frightened of the low weather ceiling around New York. His ground crew towed the *Spirit of St. Louis* from Curtiss Field to Roosevelt Field and loaded the plane. It weighed 5,250 pounds (2,381 kg), 1,000 pounds (454 kg), more than it had ever weighed before, and the engine failed to rev up to full capacity. This was a typical occurrence in bad weather. The men standing around looked worried. What if the lack of power caused Lindbergh to crash on takeoff?

Lindbergh considered the odds and decided that if he waited for the weather to clear totally, his competitors would be back in the race. He remembered all the times that he had flown his mail plane through bad weather because no flight meant no pay. He believed that the weather ceiling in and around New York was unimportant; the weather over the Atlantic was what counted. As for takeoff—well, he would finally see if his theory was correct. Would the lack of weight help?

~

He climbed into the cockpit. Years later he would write in *The Spirit of St. Louis* the following account of his takeoff (pp. 175–77):

I buckle my safety belt, pull goggles down over my eyes, turn to men at the blocks, and nod. Frozen figures leap to action. A yank on the ropes—the wheels are free. I brace myself against the left side of the cockpit, sight along the edge of the runway, and ease the throttle wide open. Now, in seconds, we'll have the answer. Action brings confidence and relief.

But except for noise and vibration, what little effect the throttle has! The plane creeps heavily forward. Several men are pushing on wing struts to help it start—pushing so hard I'm afraid the struts will buckle. How can I possibly gain flying speed? Why did I ever think air could carry such a weight? Why have I placed such reliance on a sheet of paper's curves? What possible connection is there between the intersection of a pencil's lines in San Diego and the ability of this airplane, here, now, to fly?

The Spirit of St. Louis feels more like an overloaded truck than an airplane. The tires rut through mud as though they really were on truck wheels. Even the breath of wind is pressing me down. A take-off seems hopeless; but I may as well go on for another hundred feet before giving up. Now that I've started, it's better to make a real attempt. Besides—it's just possible—

Gradually, the speed increases, maybe the runway's not too soft. Is it long enough? The engine's snarl sounds inadequate and weak, carrying its own note of mechanical frustration. There's none of the spring forward that always before proceeded the take-off into air—no lightness of wing, no excess power. The stick wobbles loosely from side to side, and slipstream puts hardly any pressure against rudder. Nothing about my plane has the magic quality of flight. But men begin stumbling off from the wing struts. We're going faster.

A hundred yards of runway passes. The last man drops off the struts. The stick's wobbling changes to lurching motion as ailerons protest unevenness of surface. How long can the landing gear stand such strain? Five thousand pounds crushing down upon it! I keep my eyes fixed on the runway's edge. I must hold the plane straight. One wheel off and the Spirit of St. Louis *would ground-loop and splinter in the mud. Controls begin to tighten against the pressure of my hand and feet. There's a living quiver in the stick. I have to push hard to hold it forward. Slight movement of the rudder keeps the nose on course. Good signs, but more than a thousand feet have passed. Is there still time, still space?*

Pace quickens—turf becomes a blur—the tail skid lifts off ground—I feel the load shifting from wheels to wings. But the runway's slipping by quickly. The halfway mark is just ahead, and I have nothing like flying speed—The engine's turning faster—smoothing out—the propeller's taking better hold—I can tell by the sound. What r.p.m.? But I can't look at instruments—I must hold the runway, not take my eyes from its edge for an instant. An inch off on stick or rudder, and my flight will end.

The halfway mark streaks past—seconds now to decide—close the throttle, or will I get off? The wrong decision means a crash—probably in flames—I pull the stick back firmly, and—The wheels leave the ground. Then I'll get off! The wheels touch again. I ease the stick forward—almost flying speed, and nearly 2000 feet of field ahead—A shallow pool on the runway—water spews up from the tires—A wing drops—lifts as I shove aileron against it—the entire plane trembles from the shock—Off

*Lindbergh's plane soars over the
United States in its history-making flight.*

again—right wing low—pull it up—Ease back onto the runway—left rudder—hold to center—must keep straight—Another pool—water drumming on the fabric—The next hop's longer—I could probably stay in air; but I let the wheels touch once more—lightly, a last bow to earth, a gesture of humility before it—Best to have plenty of control with such a load, and control requires speed.

The Spirit of St. Louis *takes herself off the next time—full flying speed—the controls taut, alive, straining—and still a thousand feet to the web of telephone wires. Now, I have to make it—there's no alternative. It'll be close, but the margin has shifted to my side. I keep the nose down, climbing slowly, each second gaining speed. If the engine can hold out for one more minute—five feet—twenty—forty—wires flash by underneath—twenty feet to spare!*

It was 7:54 A.M. Eastern Standard Time, and Charles Lindbergh was on his way to Paris.

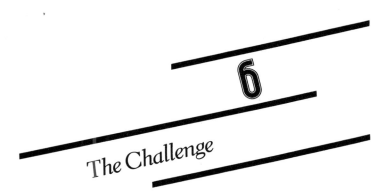

The Challenge

Lindbergh's route at the beginning of the flight took him from Long Island to Connecticut to Rhode Island. As soon as he cleared land and approached the Atlantic Ocean along the coast of Rhode Island, he cut his speed down to 100 miles per hour (160 kmph), which he knew would save him enough gas to stay in the air for fifty hours, although the flight should take no more than thirty-six. This cushion was necessary in case he got off course.

And getting off course would be an easy thing to do. Lindbergh had decided not to bring a radio on board because of its weight; he had only a compass, a sextant, and a chart. For the first time, Lindbergh would have none of the clues that he had flying over land. There was only the icy water below. He had to rely totally on the Great Arctic Circle course he had previously charted for himself. His plans had him changing course slightly

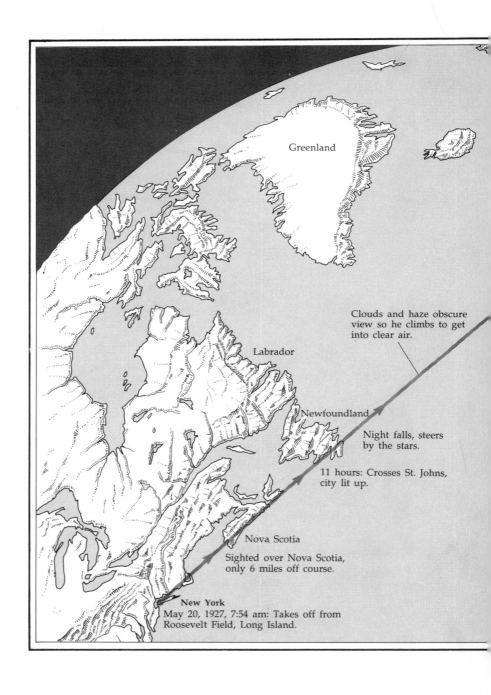

Greenland

Labrador

Newfoundland

Clouds and haze obscure
view so he climbs to get
into clear air.

Night falls, steers
by the stars.

11 hours: Crosses St. Johns,
city lit up.

Nova Scotia

Sighted over Nova Scotia,
only 6 miles off course.

New York
May 20, 1927, 7:54 am: Takes off from
Roosevelt Field, Long Island.

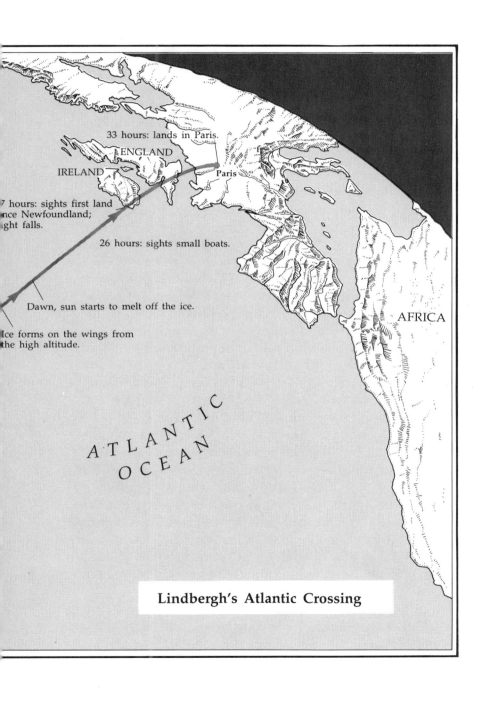

33 hours: lands in Paris.

ENGLAND

IRELAND

Paris

7 hours: sights first land
ince Newfoundland;
ght falls.

26 hours: sights small boats.

Dawn, sun starts to melt off the ice.

Ice forms on the wings from
the high altitude.

AFRICA

ATLANTIC
OCEAN

Lindbergh's Atlantic Crossing

some forty times between New York and Paris and required him to adjust these changes even more slightly based on the drift of the wind. The accuracy of his calculations would determine whether he landed in Paris or crashed in the Atlantic.

When he flew over St. John's, Newfoundland, he had been flying about eleven hours, and it was getting dark. He had not had any real sleep in almost thirty-six hours, and he was getting tired. He kept himself alert, however, because a new danger suddenly loomed ahead—icebergs. To avoid the storm, throughout much of the flight, Lindbergh flew the plane very low and close to the sea—so close, in fact, that he had to watch out for the masts of ships. Now there was the danger of hitting icebergs, and he took the plane up to avoid them. By the time he had successfully navigated them, the sky was pitch-black, and he had passed the last land he would see until he reached the coast of Ireland.

Meanwhile, although he didn't know it, the eyes of the Americas and Europe were focused on him. He was on the front page of all the major newspapers, and radio bulletins on his progress were being issued hourly in the United States, whether or not there was any new information. Announcers at sports events that Friday evening asked for a moment of silence and prayer for Lindbergh. His mother taught school as usual on Friday, but her students were disturbed both by the general excitement and by reporters outside the school building. Perhaps in an attempt to rid herself of the journalists, she allowed the *Detroit Free Press* to issue the following statement in her name:

Tomorrow, Saturday, a holiday for me, will either be the happiest day of my life, or the saddest. Saturday afternoon at three o'clock I shall begin looking for word from Paris—not before that. Perhaps I shall not worry, however, if the hours of Saturday afternoon drag along until evening. But I know I shall receive word that my boy successfully covered the long journey. . . . It will be a happy message.

In spite of this statement, the press still harassed Mrs. Lindbergh, and she was finally forced to barricade herself behind locked doors and windows for the weekend.

Her son, meanwhile, was having his own problems. Having taken the plane up to 10,500 feet (31,500 m), both to avoid icebergs and to get a look at the stars to help him navigate, he suddenly became aware that he was in the middle of an ice storm. He immediately took the plane down a little, but since he did not know how large an area the storm covered, he did not know whether or not to try to go around it. He wrote in *The Spirit of St. Louis* (p. 310):

Great cliffs tower over me, ward me off with icy walls. They belong to mountains of another world, mountains with forms that change; with summits that overhang; mountains alluring in their softness. There'd be no rending crash if my wing struck one of them. They carry a subtler death. A crash against an earthly mountain is like a sword stroke; one flash and it's over. But to plunge into these mountains of the heavens would be like stepping into quicksand. They enmesh intruders. They're barbaric in their methods. They toss you in their inner turbulence, lash you with their hailstones, poison you with freezing mist. It would be a slow death, a death one would have long minutes to struggle against, trying blindly to regain

control of an ice-crippled airplane, climbing, stalling,
diving, whipping, always downward toward the sea.

He thought of turning back, but realized that in the time
it would take to get back to Roosevelt Field, he could
reach Ireland. At that moment, while he was racked with
fatigue and indecision, the moon suddenly came out,
and by its light he was able to tell more about the clouds
through which he was trying to fly. He considered it a
good omen and decided to push on.

According to his plans for the trip, he was to
celebrate its midpoint by eating the five sandwiches Dick
Blythe had given to him, but now he found that he
wasn't hungry. The only sensation he felt was fatigue. He
told himself that it would soon be dawn and that would
make it easier to stay awake, but he was beginning to drift
into sleep. He described the sensation in *The Spirit of St.
Louis* (p. 332):

*I've lost command of my eyelids. When they start to close,
I can't restrain them. They shut, and I shake myself, and
lift them with my fingers. I stare at the instruments,
wrinkle forehead muscles tense. Lids close again regardless, stick tight as though with glue. My body has revolted
from the rule of its mind. Like salt in wounds, the light of
day brings back my pains. Every cell of my being is on
strike, sulking in protest, claiming that nothing, nothing
in the world, could be worth such effort; that man's tissue
was never made for such abuse. My back is stiff; my
shoulders ache; my face burns; my eyes smart. It seems
impossible to go on longer. All I want in life is to throw
myself down flat, stretch out—and sleep.*

*I've struggled with the dawn often enough before, but
never with such a background of fatigue. I've got to*

muster all my reserves, all the tricks I've learned, all remaining strength of mind, for the conflict. If I can hold in air and close to course for one more hour, the sun will be over the horizon and the battle won. Each ray of light is an ally. With each moment after sunrise, vitality will increase.

Lindbergh had one piece of luck. Every time he momentarily drifted off to sleep, the plane, built less for stability than for speed—would begin to wobble violently and wake him up. For nine hours he floated in and out of sleep, never soundly, and came to with a jerk whenever the plane went off course. He floated in a trancelike state, sometimes imagining that he saw things or people outside the plane, which he described in *The Spirit of St. Louis* (pp. 364–65):

While I'm staring at the instruments, during an unearthly age of time, both conscious and asleep, the fuselage behind me becomes filled with ghostly presences—vaguely outlined forms, transparent, moving, riding weightless with me in the plane. I feel no surprise at their coming. There's no suddenness to their appearance. Without turning my head, I see them as clearly as though in my normal field of vision. There's no limit to my sight—my skull is one great eye, seeing everywhere at once.

These phantoms speak with human voices—friendly, vapor-like shapes, without substance, able to vanish or appear at will, to pass in and out through the walls of the fuselage as though no wall were there. Now, many are crowded behind me. Now, only a few remain. First one and then another presses forward to my shoulder to speak above the engine's noise, and then draws back among the group behind. At times, voices come out of the air itself, clear yet far away, traveling through distances that can't be measured by the scale of human miles; familiar voices, conversing and advising on my flight, discussing problems of my navigation, reassuring me, giving me messages or importance unattainable in ordinary life. . . .

The spirits have no rigid bodies, yet they remain human in outline form—emanations from the experience of ages, inhabitants of a universe closed to mortal men. I'm on the border line of life and a greater realm beyond, as though caught in the field of gravitation between two planets, acted on by forces I can't control, forces too weak to be measured by any means at my command, yet representing powers incomparably stronger than I've ever known. . . .

Am I now more man or spirit? Will I fly my airplane on to Europe and live in flesh as I have before, feeling hunger, pain, and cold, or am I about to join these ghostly forms, become a consciousness in space, all-seeing, all-knowing, unhampered by materialistic fetters of the world?

Finally, after twenty-seven hours in the air, Lindbergh saw several small fishing boats and knew that the European coast couldn't be far away. He dipped down near one of the boats and shouted to a face in one of the portholes: "Which way is Ireland?"

No answer came, and for one moment Lindbergh wondered if he was hallucinating and imagining the boat. He convinced himself that he was not and continued to fly eastward. He was rewarded an hour later when he saw the coast of Ireland and shortly thereafter villages with people who waved at him. What Lindbergh did not yet know was that the word was out that he had made it to Ireland, and groups of people in Ireland, Cornwall, and France began to gather to cheer him on.

Finally, at almost 10 o'clock at night, thirty-three and a half hours after takeoff, he sighted the Eiffel Tower, flew around it once, and then went on to Le Bourget flying field northeast of Paris. He had some trouble finding the field but was finally convinced that a huge group of moving lights was it. He landed and suddenly realized that the lights were the largest group of people he had ever seen—and they were all there to greet him.

7

The Boy Hero

Twenty thousand men and women had waited for hours at Le Bourget to see the man who flew across the Atlantic. When they saw the plane landing, they broke through the police and military cordons to get to it, ignoring the propeller that was still whirling and the wheels that were still moving. As soon as Lindbergh stood up in the cockpit, the cheers of 20,000 voices were raised: "Lindbergh! Lindbergh! Lindbergh!" As Lindbergh climbed out of the plane, he was hoisted onto the shoulders of the nearest few men and remained there for a half hour. Finally, a souvenir hunter grabbed Lindbergh's helmet and put it on his own head. He was immediately mistaken for Lindbergh himself and carried through the crowd.

Meanwhile, three French fliers smuggled Lindbergh off the field and into their car and headed for Paris by back roads. On arriving in the city, they drove up the Champs Élysées and stopped at the Arc de Triomphe.

Section 1

"All the News That's Fit to Print."

The New York Times.

THE WEATHER
Generally fair today and tomorrow; moderate to fresh southerly winds.

Section 1

VOL. LXXVI....No. 25,320. NEW YORK, SUNDAY, MAY 22, 1927. FIVE CENTS

LINDBERGH DOES IT! TO PARIS IN 33½ HOURS; FLIES 1,000 MILES THROUGH SNOW AND SLEET; CHEERING FRENCH CARRY HIM OFF FIELD

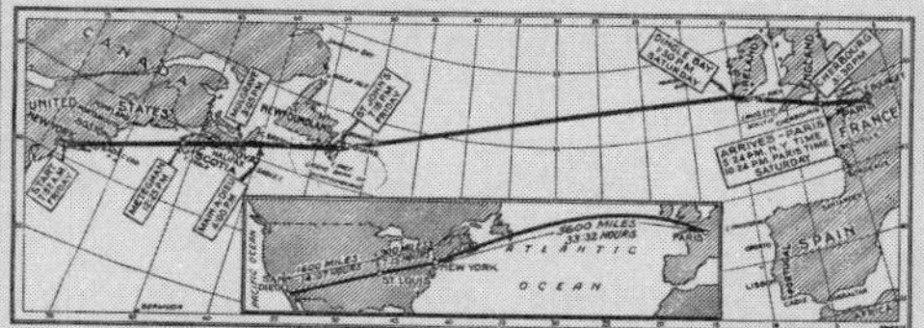

MAP OF LINDBERGH'S TRANSATLANTIC ROUTE, SHOWING THE SPEED OF HIS TRIP.

COULD HAVE GONE 500 MILES FARTHER

Gasoline for at Least That Much More—Flew at Times From 10 Feet to 10,000 Feet Above Water

ATE ONLY ONE AND A HALF OF HIS FIVE SANDWICHES

Fell Asleep at Times but Quickly Awoke—Glimpses of His Adventure in Brief Interview at the Embassy.

LINDBERGH'S OWN STORY TOMORROW.

Captain Charles A. Lindbergh was too exhausted after his arrival in Paris late last night to do more than indicate, as told below, his experiences during his flight. After he awakes today, he will narrate the full story of his remarkable exploit for readers of Monday's New York Times.

By CARLYLE MACDONALD.
Copyright, 1927, by The New York Times Company.
Special Cable to THE NEW YORK TIMES.

PARIS, Sunday, May 22.—Captain Lindbergh was discovered at the American Embassy at 2:30 o'clock this morning. Attired in a pair of Ambassador Herrick's pajamas, he sat on the edge of a bed and talked of his flight. At the last moment Ambassador Herrick had canceled the plans of the reception committee and, by unanimous consent, took the flier to the embassy in the Place d'Iena.

A staff of American doctors who had arrived at Le Bourget Field early to minister to an "exhausted" aviator found instead a bright-eyed, smiling youth who refused to be examined.

"Oh, don't bother; I am all right," he said.

"I'd like to have a bath and a glass of milk. I would feel better," Lindbergh replied when the Ambassador asked him what he would like to have.

A bath was drawn immediately and in less than five minutes the youth had disrobed in one of the embassy guest rooms, taken his bath and was out again drinking a bottle of milk and eating a roll.

"No Use Worrying," He Tells Envoy.

"There is no use worrying about me, Mr. Ambassador," Lindbergh insisted when Mr. Herrick and members of the embassy staff wanted him to be examined by doctors and then go to bed immediately.

It was apparent that the young man was too full of his experiences to want sleep and he sat on the bed and chatted with the Ambassador, his son and daughter-in-law.

By this time a corps of frantic newspaper men who had been madly chasing the airman, following one false scent after another, had finally tracked him to the embassy. In a body they descended upon the Ambassador, who received them in the salon and informed them that he had just left Lindbergh with strict instructions to go to sleep.

As Mr. Herrick was talking with the reporters his son-in-law came downstairs and said that Lindbergh had rung and announced that he did not care to go to sleep just yet and that he would be glad to see the newspaper men for a few minutes. A cheer went up from the group who dashed by Mr. Herrick and rushed upstairs.

Expected Trouble Over Newfoundland.

In the blue and gold room, with a soft light glowing, sat the conqueror of the Atlantic. He immediately stood up and held out his hands to greet his callers. THE NEW YORK TIMES correspondent being first to greet him.

"Sit down, please," urged every one with one voice, but Lindbergh only smiled again his famous boyish smile and said:

"It's almost as easy to stand up as it is to sit down."

Questions were fired at him from all sides about his trip across the ocean, but Lindbergh seemed to dismiss them all with brief, nonchalant answers.

"I expected trouble over Newfoundland because I had been warned that the situation there was unfavorable. But I got over that hazard with no trouble whatsoever."

Sleet and Snow for 1,000 Miles.

"However, it wasn't easy going. I had sleet and snow for over 1,000 miles. Sometimes it was too high to fly over and sometimes too low to fly under, so I just had to go through it as best I could.

"I flew as low as 10 feet in some places and as high as 10,000 in others. I passed no ships in the daytime, but at night I saw the lights of several ships, the night being bright and clear."

Everyone then wanted to know if the flier had been sleepy on the voyage.

"I didn't really get what you might call downright sleepy," he said, "but I think I sort of nodded several times. In fact, I could have flown half that distance again. I had enough fuel

Continued on Page Two.

LEVINE ABANDONS BELLANCA FLIGHT

Venture Given Up as Designer Splits With Him—Plane Narrowly Escapes Burning.

BYRD'S CRAFT IS NAMED

Lindbergh Cheered at Ceremony—Commander, Now Last in Field, Waits on Weather.

Through no fault of his own, Clarence D. Chamberlin, who with Bert Acosta established a world's non-stop flying record a few weeks ago, will not fly the record-breaking monoplane in an attempt to establish a second New York-Paris non-stop flight.

G. M. Bellanca, designer of the plane, and Charles S. Levine of the Columbia Aircraft Company, owner of the ship, came to the parting of the ways last night and the designer finally severed his connection with the promoter. Then Levine issued a statement that the proposed flight, which has been talked of for weeks, was off.

The statement said:

"Due to the crowning blow of Mr. Bellanca's resignation, the plane will be placed in the hangar. Mr. Bellanca's resignation causes us to abandon plans for the New York-Paris flight for the present."

At the very moment that the statement was issued the plane was near the runway at Roosevelt Field with gas tanks filled and oil and equipment aboard ready for the start for Paris.

Plane Threatened by Fire.

A few minutes later, as it was being wheeled off, preparatory to being housed for the night, it narrowly escaped being destroyed by fire. When the word came to the field that the flight was definitely off mechanics were ordered to empty one gasoline tank to lighten the machine. The gasoline spilled on the ground and while the ship was being towed away a careless spectator threw the stub of a lighted cigarette down.

In an instant there was a terrific flare and a dense burst of smoke as the gasoline blazed up.

"The Bellanca's gone," was the cry that rose from thousands of spectators who had gathered at the field.

Word was flashed to the army air station at Mitchel Field that there had been an accident and ambulances and fire-fighting apparatus were sent across the road. An ambulance from the Nassau County Hospital at Mineola was also sent to Roosevelt Field, as well as fire apparatus from Mineola.

The plane, however, was beyond the danger line and was not injured.

It had been announced that the Columbia would take off at 8 o'clock and Chamberlin was in his flying clothes ready to climb into the cockpit with the unnamed pilot who was to have accompanied him on the trip.

With the elimination of the Bellanca monoplane, only Lieut.

Continued on Page Four.

Times Wide World Photo

CAPTAIN CHARLES A. LINDBERGH,
Who Flew Alone Across the Atlantic, New York to Paris, in Thirty-three and One-half Hours.

New York Stages Big Celebration After Hours of Anxious Waiting

Harbor Craft, Factories, Fire Sirens and Radio Carry Message of the Flier's Victory Throughout the City—Theatres Halt While Audiences Cheer.

New York bubbled all day yesterday with excitement and expectancy, first yearning for word of Captain Lindbergh, then half-doubting, gaining confidence as the afternoon progressed and finally acclaiming the victory of the young aviator with street demonstrations where the crowds were thickest, in which the ancient phrase, "I told you so," was often repeated. It was evident during the day that New York had confidence in the lad from the West.

On the streets and elsewhere Lindbergh was the one topic of conversation the whole day long. In the subway, on the elevated, in trains and cars, motion-picture houses, theatres, wherever a few had gathered, or even where one man could find another to talk to, one heard "Lindbergh — Lindbergh — Lindbergh."

And such expressions as this:

"He'll make it, all right."

"Some baby!"

"Well, if he's hit Ireland, he's safe anyway."

"He's away ahead of his time."

"What's the difference in time between here and there, anyway?"

Confused On Difference in Time.

To this latter question there were some amazing answers. One woman who had the aviator's running time mixed with the difference in time between New York and Paris solemnly informed her companion that there was thirty-six hours difference in time between the cities. She said it with an air which signified: "I don't mean maybe." A surprising number of persons insisted that the difference in time was three hours.

Early in the day, even before there was any good reason why there should be definite news, the interest of the people was demonstrated in two ways. At every news stand there were little groups scanning the headlines and buying newspapers. In every newspaper office the switchboards were literally swamped with inquiries. It was not sufficient that the operator said there was no word, or, later, that Lindbergh's plane had been seen over Ireland. The inquirers wanted specific information:

"Well, when will you get the first news?" they asked. And later:

"If he's over Ireland how long will it be before he gets to Paris?"

"Is he all right?"

The questions that were asked, considering that no news could possibly come direct from Captain Lindbergh before he landed, were as surprising as the guesses at the difference in time.

The Times Gets 10,000 Phone Calls.

The telephone inquiries came from all sorts of people and all directions. Not a few rang up THE TIMES office and apologetically explained that they were on golf links or elsewhere at a distance, and hence could not

Continued on Page Three.

LINDBERGH TRIUMPH THRILLS COOLIDGE

President Cables Praise to "Heroic Flier" and Concern for Nungesser and Coli.

CAPITAL THROBS WITH JOY

Kellogg, New, MacNider, Patrick and Many More Join in Paying Tribute to Daring Youth.

Special to The New York Times.

WASHINGTON, May 21.—The triumph of Captain Charles A. Lindbergh in flying from New York to Paris without a stop created a tremendous sensation in the national capital and found immediate response in a host of official messages and statements congratulating the daring aviator upon his achievement.

President Coolidge expressed his admiration in a message transmitted through Ambassador Herrick in Paris for delivery to the young flier in person.

With a single possible exception, this city has never been more thrilled since the armistice, when Woodrow Wilson mingled with noisy thousands in celebrating the end of the war. The exception was when Walter Johnson arose from apparent defeat and won the deciding world series baseball game in 1924.

"The American people," the President said, "rejoice with me at the brilliant termination of your heroic flight. The first non-stop flight of a lone aviator across the Atlantic crowns the record of American aviation, and in bringing the greetings of the American people to France you likewise carry the assurance of our admiration of those intrepid Frenchmen, Nungesser and Coli, whose bold spirits first ventured on your exploit, and likewise a message of our continued anxiety concerning their fate."

Secretary Kellogg, in a message similarly transmitted, said:

"I heartily congratulate you on the success of your great adventure in accomplishing a non-stop flight from New York to Paris. It is a great step in the advancement of aviation. Every one in the United States is proud of your accomplishment."

Knew Lindbergh as a Boy.

In a statement issued here Mr. Kellogg referred to his personal friendship for Lindbergh, whom he has known for years through the young man's late father, a Representative in Congress from the Secretary's home State of Minnesota.

"News has just reached me," Mr. Kellogg said, "of the success of Lindbergh in completing his flight from New York to Paris. It is an achievement of which every American can justly be proud. I have known Lindbergh since he was a boy and rejoice at this culmination of his ambitions, which could only have been gained by scientific knowledge, superb courage and physique and sterling character. Our rejoicing in Lindbergh's success, however, is tempered by our continued ignorance of the fate of Nungesser and Coli, whose courage and valor have now been equaled, but cannot be surpassed."

Hanford MacNider, Acting Secre-

Continued on Page Four.

CROWD ROARS THUNDEROUS WELCOME

Breaks Through Lines of Soldiers and Police and Surging to Plane Lifts Weary Flier from His Cockpit

AVIATORS SAVE HIM FROM FRENZIED MOB OF 100,000

Paris Boulevards Ring With Celebration After Day and Night Watch—American Flag Is Called For and Wildly Acclaimed.

By EDWIN L. JAMES.
Copyright, 1927, by The New York Times Company.
Special Cable to THE NEW YORK TIMES.

PARIS, May 21.—Lindbergh did it. Twenty minutes after 10 o'clock tonight suddenly and softly there slipped out of the darkness a gray-white airplane as 25,000 pairs of eyes strained toward it. At 10:24 the Spirit of St. Louis landed and lines of soldiers, ranks of policemen and stout steel fences went down before a mad rush as irresistible as the tides of the ocean.

"Well, I made it," smiled Lindbergh, as the little white monoplane came to a halt in the middle of the field and the first vanguard reached the plane. Lindbergh made a move to jump out. Twenty hands reached for him and lifted him out as if he were a baby. Several thousands in a minute were around the plane. Thousands more broke the barriers of iron rails round the field, cheering wildly.

Lifted From His Cockpit.

As he was lifted to the ground Lindbergh was pale, and with his hair unkempt, he looked completely worn out. He had strength enough, however, to smile, and waved his hand to the crowd. Soldiers with fixed bayonets were unable to keep back the crowd.

United States Ambassador Herrick was among the first to welcome and congratulate the hero.

A NEW YORK TIMES man was one of the first to reach the machine after its graceful descent to the field. Those first to arrive at the plane had a picture that will live in their minds for the rest of their lives. His cap off, his famous locks falling in disarray around his eyes, "Lucky Lindy" sat peering out over over the rim of the little cockpit of his machine.

Dramatic Scene at the Field.

It was high drama. Picture the scene. Almost if not quite 100,000 people were massed on the east side of Le Bourget air field. Some of them had been there six and seven hours.

Off to the left the giant phare lighthouse of Mount Valerien flashed its guiding light 300 miles into the air. Closer on the left Le Bourget Lighthouse twinkled, and off to the right another giant revolving phare sent its beams high into the heavens.

Big arc lights on all sides with enormous electric glares were flooding the landing field. From time to time rockets rose and burst in varied lights over the field.

Seven thirty, the hour anounced for the arrival, had come and gone. Then 8 o'clock came, and no Lindbergh; at 9 o'clock the sun had set but then came reports that Lindbergh had been seen over Cork. Then he had been seen over Valentia in Ireland and then over Plymouth.

Suddenly a message spread like lightning, the aviator had been seen over Cherbourg. However, remembering the messages telling of Captain Nungesser's flight, the crowd was skeptical.

"One chance in a thousand!" "Oh, he cannot do it without navigating instruments!" "It's a pity, because he was a brave boy." Pessimism had spread over the great throng by 10 o'clock.

The stars came out and a chill wind blew.

Watchers Are Twice Disappointed.

Suddenly the field lights flooded their glares onto the landing ground and there came the roar of an airplane's motor. The crowd was still, then began a cheer, but two minutes later the landing glares went dark for the searchlight had identified the plane and it was not Captain Lindbergh's.

Stamping their feet in the cold, the crowd waited patiently. It seemed quite apparent that nearly every one was willing to wait all night, hoping against hope.

Suddenly—it was 10:16 exactly—another motor roared over the heads of the crowd. In the sky one caught a glimpse of a white gray plane, and for an instant heard the sound of one. Then it dimmed, and the idea spread that it was yet another disappointment.

Again landing lights glared and almost by the time they had flooded the field the gray-white plane had lighted on the far side nearly half a mile from the crowd. It seemed to stop almost as it hit the ground, so gently did it land.

And then occurred a scene which almost passed description. Two companies of soldiers with fixed bayonets and the Le Bourget field police, reinforced by Paris agents, had held the crowd in good order. But as the lights showed the plane

Lindbergh did not know that the monument before him was the tomb of France's Unknown Warrior, and as he spoke no French and his companions little English, was destined for the moment to remain in ignorance. He could tell from their attitude, however, that the spot was important to them and stood silently for a few moments before going on to the American embassy and his first real meal in two days.

The American ambassador, Myron Herrick, had been waylaid by the "fake" Lindbergh at Le Bourget and had to fight traffic all the way back to the embassy. Meanwhile, at Le Bourget, reporters were battling for telephones. The United Press had earlier made a deal at the field for exclusive use of all public telephones and had reporters in each booth to keep the phone lines from being used by other newspapers. The outraged competitors retaliated by overturning the phone booths. When Ambassador Herrick got back to the embassy, he held a press conference with Lindbergh—at 3 A.M.! Lindbergh managed to alertly answer the reporters' questions, borrowed pajamas from Herrick, and went to bed at 4:15 A.M. He had not slept in sixty-three hours.

When he awoke eight hours later, he was the most famous man in the world. From the bedroom he could still hear the cries of "Vive Lindbergh" (Long live Lindbergh) from a huge crowd standing in front of the embassy. Some 250 reporters, photographers, and movie cameramen were waiting to see him, and cables, telegrams, and presents were arriving by the score. After breakfasting—and what he had for breakfast was widely reported—he gave an interview to the *New York Times* and went out onto the front balcony of the embassy with Ambassador Herrick. His simultaneous waving of the French and American flags made the crowd go wild. He

Ambassador Herrick and Lindbergh stand
on the balcony of the American embassy while
Charles waves the French and American flags.

then held a press conference, talked over the new transatlantic phone to his mother in Detroit (she was particularly concerned that he catch up on his sleep), visited Madame Nungesser, mother of the missing French aviator, and attended an embassy party. Wherever he went, he was mobbed by crowds.

Luckily, at this point, he was a diplomat's dream. Ambassador Herrick called President Coolidge and was thrilled that Lindbergh seemed to him relaxed and unassuming in every situation. . . . "All France is deep in joy at Charles Lindbergh's brave flight," cabled the happy ambassador to the president of the United States that evening. "If we had deliberately sought a type to represent the youth, the intrepid adventure of America, and the immortal bravery of Nungesser and Coli, we could not have fared as well as in this boy of divine genius and simple courage."

When addressing an audience composed of the French minister of war and fifty of the greatest fliers in France, Lindbergh stated that, thanks to a favorable wind, this flight—west to east—had been much less difficult than the east-to-west one attempted by Nungesser and Coli and said that France should not lose hope that her two heroes would return. Herrick called Lindbergh America's "unofficial ambassador" to France and said, "This young man from out of the West brings you better than anything else the spirit of America. . . . It was needed at this time that the love of these two great peoples should manifest itself, and it is this young boy who has brought that about."

Lindbergh received the Cross of the Legion d'Honneur from the president of France and addressed the French Assembly. Half a million people lined the streets of Paris to watch him as he received their Gold Medal of the Municipality of Paris. He visited with Bleriot, who was the first Frenchman to fly the English Channel, and with the World War I marshals Foch and Joffre. He even auctioned his autograph for $1,500, in aid of French veterans. Ambassador Herrick said, "I am not a religious man, but I believe there are certain things that happen in life that can only be described as interpretation of a Divine Act. . . . Lindbergh brought you the spirit of America in a manner in which it could never be brought in a diplomatic sack."

On May 28 Lindbergh took off in the *Spirit*, circled the Arc de Triomphe once and the Eiffel Tower twice, and then dropped a message to the waiting crowd: "Good-bye, dear Paris. Ten thousand thanks for your kindness to me. Charles A. Lindbergh."

He flew to Brussels, was made a Knight of the Order of Leopold by King Albert (called "The Flying King" by his subjects because of his love for the sport), was presented to the Belgian royal family, and was presented the Belgian Aero Club gold medal, the first time the medal had ever been given to a non-Belgian. The next day the king and queen made a special trip to the airfield to see the *Spirit* and both excitedly sat in the cockpit. Queen Elizabeth, a good photographer, took several shots of Lindbergh, her husband, and the plane. Lindbergh then received the gold medal from the city of Brussels and left for England, all to the accompaniment of tumultuous crowds. When Lindbergh was passing an American soldiers' cemetery near Brussels, he dived down and dropped a wreath on one of the graves.

One hundred fifty thousand people welcomed Lindbergh to England at Croydon Aerodrome, the biggest crowd yet. During the next few days, he met the king and queen, the prime minister, the Prince of Wales (later the

Duke of Windsor)—who showed a thorough knowledge of aviation—Lord and Lady Astor, and Winston Churchill. He was given an ovation by both houses of Parliament, and he even met the future Queen Elizabeth II, only a year old, who waited in her nurse's arms. Frequently he spoke of the need for aviation to help bring the two English-speaking countries together. He attended parties, luncheons, dinners, and receptions, and placed a wreath on the Tomb of the Unknown Soldier.

In the meantime, America was becoming restless. It was in the interest of both government and business for Lindbergh to come home before the novelty of his achievement wore off, and there was widespread dismay when Ambassador Herrick informed President Coolidge that Lindbergh wished to fly the *Spirit* easterly around the world, beginning in Paris and ending in Alaska. It was only after President Coolidge as commander in chief "requested" Lindbergh to come home that the flier agreed to do so. He flew to Cherbourg, France, where the American cruiser *Memphis* was waiting, boarded it, and arrived home on June 11, 1927.

The *Memphis* was accompanied by four destroyers, two army blimps, and forty aircraft as it arrived in the navy yard at Alexandria, Virginia. Lindbergh's mother, who had traveled to Washington for the occasion and had dined with President and Mrs. Coolidge the night before, greeted him. At the Washington Monument, Coolidge made Lindbergh a colonel of the U. S. Officers' Reserve Corps and presented him with the Distinguished

Circling over the welcoming crowds in England, looking for a landing place, is Lindbergh.

Flying Cross. Lindbergh later dined with the cabinet and received a life membership of the Aeronautical Association. He then traveled to New York City, to be part of what was to be the biggest celebration of all.

Between 3 and 4 million people lined up along the streets of Manhattan. Eighteen hundred tons of paper rained down in the ticker-tape parade on Broadway. Lindbergh was presented with both the Medal of Valor and the New York State Medal of Honor. The reception was the biggest that any city has ever held—to this day. After finally receiving the long-awaited check for the Orteig Prize, Lindbergh flew to St. Louis, where he was again feted. Afterward, he made a sentimental journey to see Orville Wright in Dayton, Ohio, a gesture that Wright never forgot.

One of the many persons who had come to see Lindbergh at Curtiss Field before he flew to Paris was Harry Guggenheim, president of the Daniel Guggenheim Fund for the Promotion of Aeronautics. Born into one of the wealthiest families in America, Guggenheim had been an aviator in the navy during World War I. He became a great admirer of Lindbergh and began to advise him on financial matters. When Lindbergh was approached by George Palmer Putnam, the publisher who would later marry Amelia Earhart, to write a book on his experiences, Guggenheim provided a place of refuge at his estate on Long Island. Lindbergh worked ten to fourteen hours a day for three weeks on the story of his life and experiences, which was published under the title We and became an immediate best-seller.

Guggenheim also felt that the immense publicity Lindbergh was receiving should be used to aid the cause of aviation. He and Lindbergh decided that Lindbergh would make a three-month flying tour with the *Spirit of*

*Ticker tape rains down on the
new hero in New York City.*

St. Louis that would serve this purpose, and the Guggenheim Fund would finance it. Between July 19 and October 23, 1927, Lindbergh flew 22,350 miles (35,760 km) and visited forty-eight states. He and his entourage spent about 260 hours in the air and stopped in eighty-two cities. They flew through fog, rain, and snow, and only once were delayed. Lindbergh insisted throughout the tour that they be on time, as the purpose of the tour was to prove that flying was faster and more dependable than other modes of transportation. The tour was a success, and by 1930 America would see a 72 percent growth in the number of commercial airfields and an 84 percent increase in the amount of airmail.

According to Lindbergh in his book *Autobiography of Values* (pp. 81–83), the tour also

let me know my country as no man had ever known it before. When I returned to New York in October, the United States was represented by a new image in my mind. Instead of outlines on a paper map, I saw New England's valleys dotted by white villages, the crystal waters of Michigan's great lakes, Arizona's pastel deserts, Georgia's red cotton fields, the cascades and deep forests of the Oregon Northwest. I saw three great mountain ranges running north and south: the Appalachians, the Rockies, the Sierras—walls of a continent, holding rivers, warning off oceans. I saw waves foaming on the rocks of Maine, cloud layers pressing against Washington's Olympics. I saw California's "Golden Gate," Louisiana's delta, Florida's wide sand beaches hundreds of miles in length. . . . I circled a glacial lake in the high Sierras . . . saw wild horses galloping over Oklahoma badlands. . . . I dived into Death Valley . . . I landed in every state in the union, spoke in scores of cities, dropped messages on still more. I inspected sites for airports, talked to engineers and politicians, and tried to convince everyone who would listen that aviation had a brilliant future, in which America should lead.

Lindbergh earned $50,000 from the air tour, $25,000 for the Orteig Prize, $25,000 for endorsements from the Vacuum Oil Company, $100,000 in royalties from *We*, and large additional sums of money from other endorsements. He never minded endorsing products but insisted on choosing himself what he endorsed and what he did not.

Guggenheim was instrumental in introducing him to men who could help him with his finances, and one of them was a banker from J. P. Morgan named Dwight Morrow. Dwight Morrow was the son of an Allegheny, Pennsylvania, schoolteacher. He had attended Amherst College and had worked his way up from clerk in a lawyer's office in Pittsburgh to senior partner in the international banking firm of J. P. Morgan and Company. He was married to the former Elizabeth Cutter of Cleveland, the first female chairperson of the board of Smith College and, for a short time, interim president of the college. They and their four children lived on a large estate in Englewood, New Jersey, called Next Day Hill, and the family also had a summer home, called North Haven, on a small island off the Maine coast.

Morrow had already held several governmental positions in Washington and in Europe and in 1927 was named ambassador to Mexico. He considered that his primary responsibility was to strengthen the relationship between the Mexican and American peoples and thought that a visit from Charles Lindbergh would greatly help his cause. He persuaded the president of Mexico to formally issue an invitation. Lindbergh arrived in Mexico City on December 14, was given the keys to the city, stayed at the embassy, and was entertained at various functions throughout the city. Morrow liked Charles so much that he invited him to have his mother come down and both of them spend the Christmas holidays with his family.

~

Anne Morrow was twenty-one and a senior at Smith College when she arrived in Mexico City that Christmas. A petite brunette who was shy with strangers, Anne was, with her family, intelligent and fun. She wanted to be a writer and in fact would win both of the top literary prizes at Smith the following spring. She was smitten with Lindbergh from their first meeting and wrote in her diary (which would later be published as the book *Bring Me a Unicorn*, pp. 81–83):

I saw standing against the great stone pillar . . . a tall, slim boy in evening dress—so much slimmer, so much taller, so much more poised than I expected. A very refined face, not at all like those grinning "Lindy" pictures—a firm mouth, clear, straight blue eyes, fair hair, and nice color. Then I went down the line, very confused and overwhelmed by it all. He did not smile—just bowed and shook hands. . . .

He is very, very young and terribly shy—looked straight ahead and talked in short direct sentences which came out abruptly and clipped. You could not meet his sentences: they were statements of fact, presented such honest directness; not trying to please, just bare simple answers and statements, not trying to help a conversation

Anne Morrow Lindbergh

along. It was amazing—breathtaking. I could not speak.
What kind of boy was this? . . .

It embarrassed him to have to talk to us. He was
asked a question about the crowds here and in London.
They were not half as bad here as in Paris and London, he
said with a dry, simple-statement-of-fact statement. Sud-
denly the picture of that mad crowd, the whole nation
surging around his plane in Paris, came into mind. And
it was this boy—this shy, cool boy—and he describes that
tremendous mad scene in a few dry matter-of-fact words.
My Lord!

Daddy said we must go to bed. Abruptly, the Colonel
announced, "Well, as the Ambassador's orders are such, I
will say good night," and he shook hands quickly without
looking at us (girls) and wheeled out of the room, leaving
a perfectly amazed stillness inside of me.

Anne and Charles spent some time together during that
holiday, but no more than Lindbergh did with the other
Morrow children. Anne did make a particularly good
impression on Mrs. Lindbergh, a fact that would probably not have been lost on Lindbergh. He was supposed
to visit the Morrows at their home in Maine the
following summer but was too busy to go. He did not
actually call Anne until October 1928, at which time
they made plans to go flying from Roosevelt Field. They
stopped first at the Guggenheim estate in Sands Point,
Long Island. Anne was embarrassed because she was
dressed in a rather shabby flying outfit, not expecting an
elegant luncheon party. Afterward, she and Lindbergh
flew over New York and New Jersey, and their friendship
was cemented.

Soon Charles was giving her regular flying lessons,
and when Anne visited her mother and father in Mexico

City in November, he followed her there. Although their courtship had been carried on in great secrecy (Lindbergh had only to speak to a young woman for the newspapers to print that he was engaged to her), the press was beginning to suspect something. The embassy, however, denied that anything was going on. At the end of December 1928, Anne wrote to a family friend, "Apparently I am going to marry Charles Lindbergh. It must seem hysterically funny to you as it did to me. . . .Wish me courage and strength and a sense of humor—I will need them all."

In February 1929, the embassy announced the engagement, but no wedding date was mentioned. The Morrows soon returned to Englewood and issued invitations to a "reception" for Mrs. Lindbergh, who had been teaching for a few months at the American College in Constantinople, Turkey, on a temporary assignment. When guests arrived, they very quickly realized that they were attendees at the wedding of Charles Lindbergh and Anne Morrow. After the short service, the bride and groom cut the wedding cake, drank ginger ale, then changed their clothes and left the estate under the unsuspecting eyes of the gathered reporters. The marriage was not announced to the press until the couple had been given enough time to make their escape.

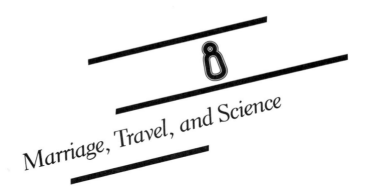

Marriage, Travel, and Science

Charles and Anne Lindbergh's marriage was to last forty-five years and would be an example to others, but the first year was an adjustment for both individuals. This adjustment was made more difficult by the intrusion of the press, which was becoming an increasing burden on Lindbergh. For ten days after their marriage, the couple sailed undisturbed along the Maine coast but were finally spotted by a flying boat complete with reporters and cameramen. Almost immediately a motorboat with the press aboard began circling the boat, and the press on board called out that they would leave if the Lindberghs would pose for one picture. Lindbergh refused, and the press boat continued to circle for hours, causing Anne to become seasick. They were finally able to escape, but some of the honeymoon glow was gone.

Lindbergh himself was becoming increasingly tired of the attention. He was unable to go anywhere without crowds forming, and fans seemed to abandon the most basic rules of polite behavior when he was around. If he ate in a restaurant, people would come over to the table and ask for autographs. Once a woman actually looked into his mouth to see what he was eating! He could not even send his clothing out to a laundry, as it would be taken by fans.

Lindbergh became obsessed with the "evils of the press." He told his new wife, "Never say anything you wouldn't want shouted from the housetops, and never write anything you would mind seeing on the front page of a newspaper." Because Anne was so in love with him, she tried to follow his directives. "But what a sacrifice to make never to speak or write deeply or honestly!" she would write years later. Both of them sometimes resorted to strategies that seemed silly to others. Shopping in a Connecticut town with her sister Constance, Anne and Charles decided to disguise themselves by dressing unattractively. But Anne complained that people were still staring at them. "Yes, dear," said Constance, who had dressed normally. "They're wondering why such a nice girl is going around with such awful hicks."

But the press was not the only problem. Anne's family was conservative, wealthy, literary, and cultured. They placed enormous emphasis on education. Lindbergh was a college dropout with little or no interest in art, music, or literature, subjects that were the soul and breath of Anne. At one point during their courtship, she was horrified when he mentioned that his favorite poet was Robert Service, who was popular but not highly regarded. At this time, she herself was a bit sheltered, having only an understanding of those persons in her own social sphere. Suddenly, she was exposed to all kinds of people, and she was not always impressed. After meeting some housewives in Kansas City, she wrote, "The average noncollege woman can talk for hours without a letup."

The couple, however, had at least one thing going for them. Charles wanted a wife who would accompany him on his adventures, and Anne discovered that she loved flying and accompanying him. She set about learning everything she needed to know in order to be a true helpmate to Lindbergh on his flights—not only piloting itself but also how to operate a radio, send Morse code, and navigate. Charles was a stern taskmaster when he was teaching her to fly, with classes sometimes lasting up to ten hours a day. She never complained and by April of 1930 was able to accompany him as a qualified navigator and radio operator on a record-breaking transcontinental flight.

While in California to pick up their plane for this flight, they met for the first time Amelia Earhart, who apologized profusely for the "Lady Lindy" title the press had given her. Anne, however, agreed with the press that Earhart and Lindbergh greatly resembled each other, and more than physically. "She [Earhart] is the most amazing person—," Anne wrote, "just as tremendous as C., I think . . . she has the clarity of mind, impersonal eye, coolness of temperament, balance of a scientist. Aside from that, I like her." Earhart, on her part, was greatly impressed by Anne—by her knowledge of art and literature and by her ability to participate in Charles's flying exploits as well as make a good home for him. She was also impressed by Anne's ability to stand up to Charles upon occasion. Earhart's husband, George Putnam, told of one incident in his book *Soaring Wings* (pp. 183–84):

Anne, the Colonel, and AE were fellow guests at the home of Jack Maddux in Los Angeles . . . one night they were

*Anne became a skilled navigator and
radio operator and frequently
accompanied Charles on flights.*

sitting about close to the icebox. Anne and AE were drinking buttermilk. Lindbergh, standing behind his wife munching on a tomato sandwich, had the sudden impulse to let drops of water fall in a stream on his wife's shoulder from a glass in his other hand.

Anne was wearing a sweet dress of pale blue silk. Water spots silk. AE observed a growing unhappiness on Anne's part—but no move toward rebellion, not even any murmur of complaint. AE often said that Anne Lindbergh is the best sport in the world.

Then Anne rose and stood by the door, with her back to the others, and her head resting on her arm. AE thought, with horror, that the impossible had come to pass, and that Anne was crying. But Anne was thinking out a solution to her problem, and the instant she thought it out, she acted upon it. At once—and with surprising thoroughness.

With one comprehensive movement she swung around and—quite simply—threw the contents of her glass of buttermilk straight over the Colonel's blue serge suit. It made a simply marvelous mess! Lindbergh's look of utter amazement changed into a tremendous grin, and he threw his head up and shouted with laughter. The joke, very practical, was certainly on him!

AE always suspected that no more of Anne's wardrobe ever got spotted—at least in that way.

Earhart wrote a magazine article about Anne in which she said: "She is an extremely feminine, gentle personage, without mannerisms, pretenses or superiorities. . . . Hers is a reticence of genuine modesty without aloofness." Lindbergh she found more difficult socially but greatly admired both his flying capabilities and his strength of character.

When the couple took off on a record-breaking flight in the spring of 1930, Anne was seven months pregnant. The press had gotten wind of this, and there was even more interest in this flight as a result. There were storm conditions that Lindbergh was determined to ignore, because he wanted to prove that flying above the clouds made it possible to fly in all kinds of weather. Unfortunately, he had to take the plane to a height that was very difficult for Anne in her condition, and she was ill for a substantial portion of the flight. Despite this, they broke the transcontinental record, and Anne was safely delivered of a baby boy on her birthday, June 22. He was named Charles Augustus, after his father.

Once the excitement of the baby's birth had died down, the press seemed to leave the Lindberghs alone for a while. Anne was free to enjoy her baby, her family, and her friends without worrying about flashbulbs going off in her face, and Charles could go into New York to handle his business affairs without being followed by hordes of photographers.

These trips were necessary because he was rapidly becoming very busy with various enterprises. Transcontinental Air Transport (TAT) hired him as chief technical director at $10,000 a year and also gave him 25,000 shares of stock at half the market price. Pan-American Airways also retained him as a technical adviser at $10,000 a year plus giving him numerous stock options. He made additional money through his association by marriage with the firm of J. P. Morgan, which was able to put a number of lucrative opportunities his way. On his way to becoming a millionaire, Lindbergh hired a family friend of the Morrows, Colonel Henry C. Breckinridge, as his legal and financial adviser. This freed him to attend the numerous conferences concerning TAT transcontinental routes, to fly to South America to check a route for Pan-American Airways, and to work with Dr. Alexis Carrel, a French biologist.

Dr. Carrel had won the Nobel Prize in 1912 for his discovery of a method of suturing blood vessels during surgery. He was currently working on artificial transplants, and Lindbergh began to work with him at the Rockefeller Institute in New York. Anne's sister Elisabeth had a heart problem, which doctors had told Lindbergh could not be corrected because her heart couldn't be stopped long enough to perform surgery. Lindbergh wondered if an artificial heart couldn't keep a patient going while surgery was performed. With Dr. Carrel, he began work on a blood pump for an artificial heart, called a perfusion pump.

He also worked with Robert H. Goddard, a scientist who, as early as 1916, had been interested in rockets. In 1929 Goddard had fired a liquid-powered rocket into the air in Auburn, Massachusetts, and it had risen to a height of 100 feet (300 m). Goddard was convinced that rockets could be used in aviation, in defense, and in a future space program, and in a short period of time he had convinced Lindbergh as well. Unfortunately, he was unable to convince the U.S. government, who maintained that he was a crank. Luckily, Lindbergh was able to convince his friend Harry Guggenheim that the work was worth pursuing, and Guggenheim's foundation gave $140,000 to enable Goddard to move his work to a

Dr. Alexis Carrel, French biologist, and the perfusion pump he and Lindbergh devised.

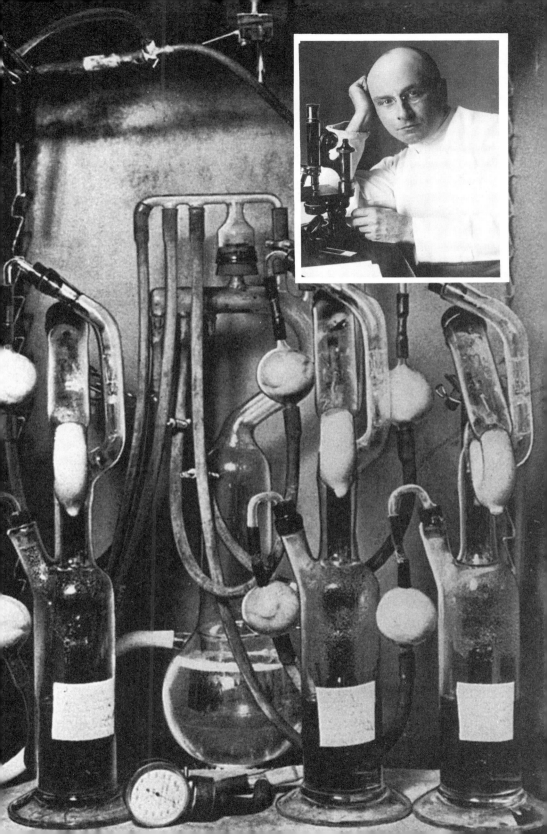

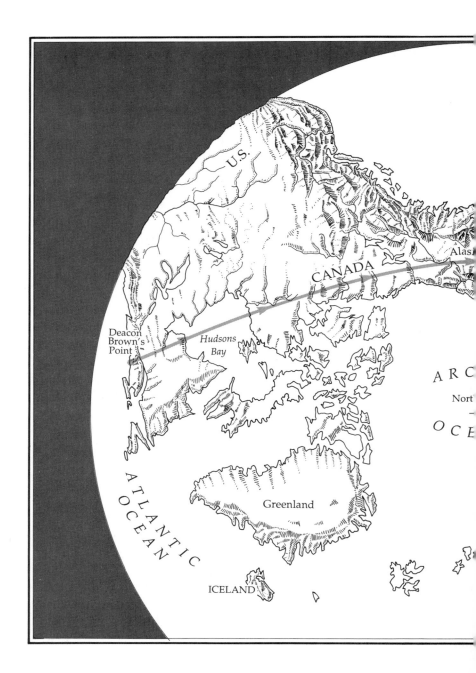

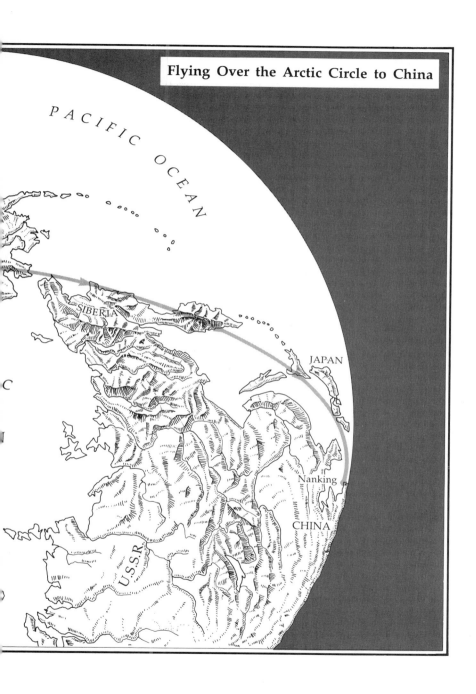

PACIFIC OCEAN

SIBERIA

JAPAN

Nanking

CHINA

U.S.S.R.

testing site in New Mexico. Years later, his work would be used in both military defense and the space program.

~

In July 1930, Charles and Anne began a trip they had been planning for some time. Their flight would take them by way of the Great Circle and over the Arctic Sea to China. They flew from the Morrow summer home— Deacon Brown's Point in Maine—across Hudson's Bay, to the Seward Peninsula, into Alaska, across the Bering Strait to Siberia, to Japan, and finally to Nanking, China. For much of their journey, they flew over places where no plane had ever been. Their plane, the *Sirius*, had pontoons on it for landing in water, which was fortunate because when they reached Nanking, they discovered that the Yangtze River had flooded. Lindbergh was able to offer his plane for famine relief. On a trip to one village, carrying medical supplies to a doctor, he nearly lost both his plane and his life. Starving Chinese assumed there was food in the plane and were in danger of sinking it when Lindbergh fired a gun over their heads, frightening them off.

In Shanghai, the Lindberghs kept the plane aboard a British aircraft carrier. One day, the plane began to capsize when it was being lowered into the water with both Lindberghs in it. The couple was forced to dive overboard, and the *Sirius* sustained extensive damage. Shortly after, Anne received word from her mother that her father, Dwight Morrow, was dead of a cerebral hemorrhage. She was heartsick, and also missed her baby; the adventure was gone from the trip. As radio operator—and an excellent one—she was essential to the trip, and Charles did not wish to continue without her. He shipped their plane to San Francisco for repairs, and they sailed home.

~

Shortly afterward, the Lindberghs moved to a new home located near Hopewell in southern New Jersey. Their house was not huge but large enough for the Lindbergh family and their servants and had been picked primarily for its isolation and difficulty of access. Anne was having a difficult winter. She was pregnant again, was feeling unwell, and was depressed about the death of her father. Thus, they still spent weekdays at Next Day Hill with her mother and weekends only at the new house. Then in late winter, tragedy struck.

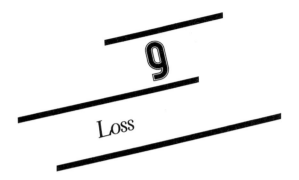

9

Loss

On one particular weekend in late February 1932, all three Lindberghs were sick with colds. When Charles left for appointments in New York City the following Monday, he told Anne that she and the baby should probably stay at home for another day. On Tuesday, both Anne and the baby were better, so the decision was made to leave for Next Day Hill on Wednesday, March 2. On Tuesday night, Charles returned from New York about 9 o'clock and had dinner with Anne. She and the nurse, Betty Gow, had earlier put the baby to bed. He slept in a second-floor bedroom. After dinner, Charles was downstairs reading and Anne was in her bedroom. Suddenly, Betty Gow came in. "Mrs. Lindbergh, do you have the baby?" she asked.

"Why, no," Anne said, "I don't have him."

The two women immediately went to see if Charles had him in his study. He didn't and ran upstairs to the nursery. The three searched it and the rest of the house. When the child was nowhere to be found, Lindbergh turned to his wife and said, "Anne, they have stolen our baby." He then found a ransom note on the window sill.

Lindbergh made a quick search of the long drive leading to the road and the road itself, but found nothing. Meanwhile, Anne, Betty Gow, and Elsie Whateley, the housekeeper, again searched all of the rooms. When Lindbergh returned, he called the New Jersey state police and his attorney, Colonel Henry Breckenridge. The police, on arriving, were directed to the ransom note on the window sill, but they would allow no one to touch it until a fingerprint expert arrived. A state trooper soon showed up and dusted the note for fingerprints, but was unable to find any. Written in pencil, the note said:

> Dear Sir!
> Have 50.000 $ redy 25 000 $ in
> 20 $ bills 1.5000 $ in 10 $ bills and
> 10000 $ in 5 $ bills. After 2–4 days
> we will inform you were to deliver
> the Mony.
> We warn you for making
> anyding public or for notify the Police
> the chld is in gute care.
> Indication for all letters are
> singnature
> and 3 holds.
> [*The "holds" were two circles linked
> together, with an oval within them.*]

The growing numbers of policemen were joined by hordes of reporters and photographers. By noon the next

Above: Charles Lindbergh, Jr.
Top right: aerial view of the Lindbergh
home in Hopewell, New Jersey
Bottom right: reporters and photographers
gather near the Lindbergh home, in an
almost carnival atmosphere, to cover
the Lindbergh baby kidnapping.

day, it was estimated that no less than 400 of the press were prowling the grounds of the Lindbergh estate, probably obliterating any footprints that the kidnappers might have left. Lindbergh was afraid that their presence would prevent further contact with the kidnappers and therefore asked that they remove themselves to Trenton, New Jersey. Many only went as far as the town of Hopewell, where, as Ludovic Kennedy would later write in his book *The Airman and the Carpenter*, they "took over the local hotel and kept it open night and day, paid inflated sums for beds in private houses, filled the waiting rooms in the railroad station with copying and transmitting equipment, obliged the telephone exchange to treble its capacity, trampled over private gardens, drove recklessly down the village street, and asked impertinent questions of anyone likely to provide the most trivial copy." The kidnapping was one of the top stories of all times, eclipsing all other current news, including the war between China and Japan, the growing problems in Hitler's Germany, and congressional attempts to pass a new—and important—tax bill. The International News Service sent out 50,000 words the first day and 30,000 the second; the Associated Press, normally very restrained, sent out 10,000 a day. Much of the information was inaccurate and some of it purposely fabricated. Interviews were conducted with hundreds of persons—everyone who lived within a few miles of the Lindbergh home, every carpenter who had worked on the building of their house, the oldest resident of Hopewell, the local clergy, even all local telephone operators.

Meanwhile, the police had sealed off all exits from New Jersey, and customs officials began a search of all boats along the New Jersey shoreline. People were so upset by what had happened that many made private searches, going through unoccupied houses and isolated areas searching for the baby. Hundreds of reports came in from all over the country from people who claimed that they had seen the baby with someone in a public place. Subsequent investigations usually revealed the supposed Lindbergh baby as the real child of the people with whom he or she had been seen. Churches and synagogues throughout the country offered prayers for the baby's safe return, as did audiences in theaters and even in Madison Square Garden. Presidents and kings sent words of encouragement and sympathy, and the Lindberghs received thousands of letters from ordinary citizens.

At this time, unfortunately, kidnapping was still a state offense rather than a federal offense, and therefore the FBI was barred from the case. Consequently, the group that was most up-to-date in large-scale crime detection was unable to use their expertise and experience. Instead, the investigation was handled by the New Jersey state police, led by Colonel Norman Schwartzkopf who, although a West Point graduate and veteran of World War I, had little actual police or crime detection experience. He was determined to conduct the case with little or no outside assistance and several times refused to utilize methods that were more modern than those more familiar to him.

Lindbergh quickly informed Schwartzkopf that his primary concern was for the safe return of his baby and that he wanted the force's assurance that nothing would be done to hinder that, even if it tied up the investigation. The arrest of the criminals was to be secondary. Lindbergh further stated that his representatives—or indeed any representative that the kidnappers chose—would be prepared to meet them at any time and place, and all arrangements would be kept confidential.

~

Even the underworld tried to become involved in the case. Famous Chicago gangster Al Capone, who was then in jail for tax evasion, made the statement that he could arrange for the boy's release in ten days—if he were let out of jail. Lindbergh himself sought the help of one Morris (Mickey) Rosner, who had many underworld contacts, and Rosner made many inquiries, but to no avail. Meanwhile, Lindbergh received a second note from the kidnappers, complaining about the publicity and warning that nothing would happen until everything calmed down. They also raised the ransom demand to $70,000. Oddly, there was no threat to harm the baby if these demands were not met, the reason being unclear until later.

After receiving this note, Lindbergh notified the press that Rosner and two cohorts would be his contacts with the kidnappers. This announcement enraged many Americans, who felt that minor-league gangsters were hardly the persons to represent their young hero. Ultimately, however, it did not matter, because despite numerous forays into the underworld, nothing was discovered, and the kidnappers made no attempt to contact Rosner or his cronies. Finally, Rosner stated that he believed the work to be that of an amateur, not a professional, criminal. Meanwhile the kidnappers had chosen their own contact.

Dr. John F. Condon was a seventy-two-year-old retired teacher from the Bronx in New York City. For many years, he had contributed to the *Bronx Home News*, which had a circulation of 100,000. After the kidnapping, he wrote an impassioned letter to the newspaper, offering himself as a go-between for the criminals. The evening after the letter was published, Condon received the following letter:

Dear Sir:
If you are willing to act as go-between in Lindbergh cace please follow stricly instruction. Handel incloced letter personaly to Mr. Lindbergh. It will explain everyding. Don't tell anyone about it. As son we find out the Press or Police is notifyd everding are cansell and it will be a further delay. Affter you gett the money from Mr. Lindbergh put these 3 words in the New York American

Mony is redy

After that we will give you further instruction. Don't be affrait we are not out fore your 1000 $ keep it. Only act stricly. Be at home every night between 6–12 by this time you will hear from us.

Condon got in touch with Bill Thayer, a friend of the Lindberghs, who was involved in the investigation. Thayer asked him to read the note to be given to Lindbergh, which said:

Dear Sir, [*Condon read*] Mr. Condon may act as go-between. You may give him the $70,000 $ make one packet. the size will bee about [here Condon explained there was a drawing of a box with its dimensions—seven by six by fourteen inches—printed alongside] we have notifyt you allredy in what kind of bills. We warn you not to set any trapp in any way. If you, or someone els will notify the Police ther will be a further delay, affter we have the mony in hand we will tell you where to find your boy. You may have a airplane rdy it is about 150 mil awy. But befor telling you the adr. a delay of 8 houers will be between.

Thayer asked Condon to come out to Hopewell, where he was met by Breckenridge and Lindbergh. Lindbergh believed the notes were genuine and asked Condon to spend the night. The next day Condon, acting as intermediary, placed an ad in the *New York American* saying that the money was ready. The day after that Condon got a phone call telling him that the message had been received and that instructions would be forthcoming. The following night he received a message to go to a frankfurter stand about a mile away and look under a large round stone. He did so and was told to go to the main entrance of the Woodlawn Cemetery, a well-known spot where F. W. Woolworth, Jay Gould, Joseph Pulitzer, Herman Melville, and other famous people were buried. Condon and a friend went there, and Condon met with a man who called himself "John," who told him that the baby was in good health and was on a boat six hours away. He also told Condon that the gang, which consisted of four men and two women, would not be sending any more letters but would send the baby's sleeping clothes to prove that they had him. Condon agreed to put an ad in the next Sunday's *Bronx Home News*, "Baby is Alive and Well. Money is Ready," to indicate that the deal was on.

Condon followed these instructions, and several days later a sleeping outfit was delivered to his house. Lindbergh came the next day and pronounced it to be that of Charles, Jr. An attached note stated that $70,000 should be paid without sight of the baby first. If the Lindberghs agreed, an ad should be placed in the *New*

York American saying, "I accept Mony is redy." The note promised that eight hours after receiving the money the kidnappers would notify the parents where to find the baby. These instructions were followed, and on April 2 Condon received instructions to go to a greenhouse and florist shop in the Bronx with the money. Lindbergh accompanied him. At the shop there was another note waiting, telling Condon to go to a nearby cemetery. He did so but found no one waiting. He was about to leave when a voice called out, "Hey, Doc!"

Condon recognized the man approaching him as the earlier contact. They exchanged money and the note, and the man quickly ran away. Condon rejoined Lindbergh, and they opened the envelope and read:

> the boy is on Boad Nelly
> it is a small Boad 28 feet
> long, two person are on the
> Boad, the are innosent.
> you will find the Boad between
> Horseneck Beach and gay Head
> near Elizabeth Island

The following day, Lindbergh flew from Bridgeport, Connecticut, to investigate the area around the Elizabeth Islands between Martha's Vineyard and Cape Cod. He spent several days combing the New England coast for a boat called *Nelly*, but with no success. Finally, realizing that he had been tricked, he returned to his home.

~

For the first few days after the kidnapping, Lindbergh looked like "a desperate man—I could not speak to him, I was afraid to," according to Anne. After the initial shock, however, he kept himself busy by helping with the investigation. Anne was less lucky. Unable to assist in the pursuit and further immobilized by her advancing pregnancy, she was marooned in the house in Hopewell. Not that she was by any means alone. "Bedlam," she called it in her diary. "Hundreds of men stamping in and out, sitting everywhere, on the stairs, on the pantry sink. The telephone goes all day and night. People sleep all over the floors on newspapers and blankets. I have never seen such self-sacrifice and energy." She poured her thoughts and feelings into her diary and was consoled by Charles, her mother, and some of the thousands of letters that were pouring in.

Others were less comforting. Almost half were from cranks, saying that the Lindberghs were being punished for their sins. Sometimes people who had found out what the Lindbergh telephone number was would call saying that they had the child and then make obscene comments. Often, politicians or film stars, for publicity, would announce to the press that they possessed an important clue. Cranks also occasionally got into the Hopewell house by insisting that they had specific information. One began to recite Shakespeare to Anne, and another accused her and Charles of killing the baby themselves.

The worst hoax was perpetrated by a Norfolk, Virginia, boat builder named John Hughes Curtis, who convinced Lindbergh that the boy was on a boat off the eastern shore. Thinking that it could be the *Nelly*, Lindbergh spent almost three weeks with Curtis at sea, looking for the boat. This adventure was finally ended by tragic news. Word came that the baby's body had been found in the woods near the Hopewell home. Curtis confessed that he had deceived Lindbergh for the publicity. Lindbergh said one word to him—"Filth"—and walked out of the room.

Betty Gow had already identified the body, but Lindbergh insisted upon viewing it himself when he arrived home the next day. He stated that it was the body of his child, went with the police to the crematorium at Linden, New Jersey, where the child's body was cremated, and then went home to his wife. Later, she would describe him as a "wall to lean on."

The two differed, however, in their feelings as to what to do next. Anne felt that it was important that they move forward and try to put the incident behind them. Charles, however, was obsessed with finding the killer or killers. He even worked with the police to try to reconstruct the crime, to determine whether the baby had been killed deliberately or accidentally. He could talk of nothing else. "I feel as if it were a poison working in my system, this idea of the crime," Anne wrote in her diary. "How deep will it eat into our lives?"

10

Escape

Anne Lindbergh gave birth to her second son, Jon, on August 16, 1932, at her mother's apartment in New York City. Both she and Charles were extremely concerned about the privacy and safety of their new baby, and Charles issued a statement to the press:

Mrs. Lindbergh and I have made our home in New Jersey. It is natural that we should wish to continue to live there near our friends and interests. Obviously, however, it is impossible for us to subject the life of our second son to the publicity which we feel was in large measure responsible for the death of our first. We feel that our children have the right to grow up normally with other children. Continued publicity will make this impossible. I am appealing to the Press to permit our children to live the lives of normal Americans.

Both Anne and Charles had enormous feelings of bitterness toward the press, and one of the first things that Charles did after the birth was to buy a huge German shepherd, which they called Thor, as a watchdog. Thor could open and close doors on command, take orders in a whisper, carry messages back and forth between Charles and Anne, retrieve objects, take the other family dogs for a walk with a leash, leap fences, and, most importantly, guard the family. He was especially protective of Anne and would even swim out to her in the ocean and make her come back to shore when he felt she had gone out too far. He was also fiercely protective of the baby.

Originally, Thor had been bought to protect the family at the Hopewell house, but the Lindberghs did not stay there long after the birth of their second baby. The place held too many painful memories and was obviously not safe. Ultimately, they would give it to the state of New Jersey as a home for boys. In the meantime, they moved into Next Day Hill with Mrs. Morrow, where there were plenty of guards and servants. This proved to be a mixed blessing, however. Mrs. Morrow was an energetic and vivacious woman who filled her life with various meetings, charities, projects, and people of all kinds. Anne and Charles felt safe there but realized that it could be only a temporary stop, since both needed privacy and a home of their own.

Charles did involve himself in some projects during that period. He began to work again with Dr. Alexis Carrel on a blood pump for an artificial heart and also to plot new routes for TAT and Pan American Airways. In the spring of 1933 he and Anne made a transcontinental flight to Los Angeles and also checked out TAT's new route for its cargo plane service.

A much more taxing, and also more important, trip lay in store for them. In the summer of 1933, they left on a Pan American Airways flight to the North Atlantic. The purpose of the flight was to provide the scientific data necessary to help Pan Am plan regular passenger service across the Atlantic.

The Lindberghs were gone for almost six months. They went to Greenland, Iceland, Scandinavia, Russia, and Britain. They then flew to Spain, West Africa, Brazil, and across the Caribbean to Miami and then New York. Since most of the places they went to had only rudimentary airstrips and crude communications systems, it was necessary to be as independent as possible. Extra fuel, food, and emergency equipment had to be carried at all times. Also, alternative routes had to be planned for all parts of the trip, since accurate information about the weather and landing conditions of any one destination was hard to come by. The extra weight that they carried posed some new problems for the Lindberghs, for they needed better and stronger winds for takeoff than they had ever needed before. The lack of wind became particularly important on their homeward journey. They also encountered a variety of other difficulties throughout the six months, from blizzards to sandstorms. Despite their difficulties, the trip was beneficial because it was the first time that Anne Lindbergh was able to shake herself out of the lethargy and sadness she had felt since the death of the baby. As an expert radio operator she was an enormous help to Charles, and she was later to chronicle their experiences in a book titled *Listen! the Wind*.

When they arrived in Miami, there was a welcoming telegram from President Roosevelt:

WELCOME HOME AND CONGRATULATIONS UPON
THE SUCCESSFUL COMPLETION OF THIS ANOTHER
FLIGHT MADE BY YOU IN THE INTEREST AND FOR
THE PROMOTION OF AMERICAN AVIATION STOP I
HOPE THAT OUT OF THE SURVEY YOU HAVE MADE
NEW AND VALUABLE PRACTICAL AIDS TO AIR TRANS-
PORTATION WILL COME STOP FRANKLIN D
ROOSEVELT

The Lindberghs replied:

THANK YOU VERY MUCH FOR YOUR MESSAGE STOP
OUR TRIP HAS MADE US MORE CONFIDENT THAN
EVER OF THE FEASIBILITY OF ESTABLISHING REGU-
LAR TRANSATLANTIC AIRLINES IN THE NEAR FUTURE
STOP ANNE LINDBERGH CHARLES LINDBERGH

Unfortunately, this cordial relationship was not to last. A
Senate committee soon after discovered that the Hoover
government had conspired with the larger air companies
to squeeze the smaller companies out of competition
with them for airmail contracts. For instance, Hoover's
postmaster general had awarded a contract for the transport of mail between New York and Washington to a big
company for three times the bid of a smaller, rejected
company. In an investigation of the larger companies, a
number of persons were found to have profited financially
in their dealings with them, and some of these persons
had governmental connections. One name mentioned
was Lindbergh's.

Lindbergh was furious. He immediately opened up
his financial records and invited the committee to view
their contents. His records revealed that, indeed, he had
made a great deal of money through TAT and Pan Am,

but they also revealed that he had been working for the companies as a technical consultant at the time, and nothing indicated that he had used his governmental ties to secure airmail contracts for these companies. Because of his association with the larger air companies, it was assumed that he would leap to their defense, but he probably recognized that there had been some double dealing and wisely refrained from becoming further involved in the controversy after he had proved his own innocence.

Meanwhile, President Roosevelt felt compelled to cancel the current airmail contracts, as they had been obtained in an unfair manner. He decided to do this immediately, rather than renegotiate when the contracts ran out in a few months. This was a mistake. The airmail job, temporarily given to the Army Air Corps, was a difficult one. The Army Air Corps was woefully unprepared for it. It was unused to night flying, flying blind, airmail routes, and bad weather. In one week, there were five deaths, six serious injuries, and eight wrecked planes. Lindbergh, who had seen the disaster coming, was furious and sent the following telegram to Roosevelt:

YOUR ACTION YESTERDAY AFFECTS FUNDAMEN-
TALLY THE INDUSTRY TO WHICH I HAVE DEVOTED
THE LAST TWELVE YEARS OF MY LIFE. THEREFORE,
I RESPECTFULLY PRESENT TO YOU THE FOLLOWING:
THE PERSONAL BUSINESS LIVES OF AMERICAN CITI-
ZENS HAVE BEEN BUILT AROUND THE RIGHT TO JUST
TRIAL BEFORE CONVICTION, YOUR ORDER OF CAN-
CELLATION OF ALL AIRMAIL CONTRACTS CONDEMNS
THE LARGEST PORTION OF OUR COMMERCIAL AVIA-
TION WITHOUT JUST TRIAL. . . . YOUR PRESENT
ACTION DOES NOT DISCRIMINATE BETWEEN INNO-

President Franklin D. Roosevelt

CENCE AND GUILT AND PLACES NO PREMIUM ON
HONEST BUSINESS. . . . THE CONDEMNATION OF
COMMERCIAL AVIATION BY CANCELLATION OF ALL
AIRMAIL CONTRACTS AND THE USE OF THE ARMY ON
COMMERCIAL AIRLINES WILL UNNECESSARILY AND
GREATLY DAMAGE ALL AMERICAN AVIATION.

Roosevelt realized that he had made an error and immediately cut back on flights until the weather improved. He also requested that Congress enact legislation by which new airmail contracts would be carefully scrutinized. He tried to placate Lindbergh by offering him a place on a war department board to review the training program of the Air Corps. However, Lindbergh, still seething and not wanting to be a part of the New Deal administration, refused. The controversy died down, but neither Lindbergh nor Roosevelt forgot it. It would not be the last time that they would be in conflict with each other.

Luckily, good things were happening in aviation at that time, also. Lindbergh worked with airplane designer Igor Sikorsky to design and build the new Pan Am Clippers, which would be used on the first regular Atlantic and South American passenger flights. He also took one of them up when it was ready and broke the record for speed for transport seaplanes. At the same time, regular overnight transcontinental service was established. Lindbergh could take a great deal of credit for these accomplishments.

Unfortunately, he had little time to enjoy them. While he and Anne were visiting her sister Elisabeth and her husband in California in September of 1934, he received word that a Bronx carpenter, Bruno Richard Hauptmann, had been arrested for the kidnapping and murder of his son. Immediately, the Lindberghs left for

New Jersey and the extradition proceedings. Anne had hoped that once these were over, they would get on with their lives. But Lindbergh wanted to be at the trial itself.

The trial opened in Flemington, New Jersey, on January 3, 1935. Three hundred reporters descended on the quiet town and turned it temporarily into a three-ring circus, according to Leonard Mosley, who was a copy boy during the trial and who later wrote in Lindbergh's biography (p. 188):

Pictures float back into the mind of that small, clean Andrew Wyeth town of painted houses and churches reeling before the invasion of people who didn't belong. Continuous publicity in the press had whipped interest to a perfervid pitch, and everyone wanted to be there. Three hundred reporters, sketch writers, and sob sisters had flocked into Flemington and had taken over the Union Hotel, across the street from the courthouse, and every rooming house in town was bulging at the seams. Not all of the newsmen had tickets for the proceedings and were avid for ancillary and off-beat stories; and once more the flacks were there to cater to them, as they had done after the kidnaping. They shipped their clients, starlets, strip teasers, politicians, cafe society debutantes, across the river and set them loose among the reporters and photographers, and any marginal comment about the crime was good for a story and a picture. The pages of the newspapers were open, and everything else happening in the world took second place.

It was possible to buy a "certified veritable lock of hair from Baby Lindbergh," or an "autographed" photograph of Lindbergh himself. Even the principal attorneys joined in the carnival atmosphere by attacking each other in the press at the end of every day in court. It was obvious from their behavior that they were as interested in the publicity the case generated as they were in seeing justice done.

This was particularly true in the case of the defense attorney, Edward J. Reilly. There have been endless debates as to whether or not Hauptmann was guilty of the kidnapping, but most experts agree that, at any rate, he definitely did not receive a fair trial. The evidence against him, although strong, was primarily circumstantial. The ladder that had been used to climb to the window of the baby's room was found to have been made of the same wood as wood found in Hauptmann's garage. Moreover, he did pass some of the ransom money, whose serial numbers had been traced. After he was arrested, more of the money was found hidden in his garage. He always maintained that he had received the money from a former partner, now dead, and that his only sin was in not reporting gold certificate money. Had the prosecution been pitted against a competent defense attorney, it would have had difficulty in proving beyond a shadow of a doubt that Hauptmann was involved. He had an alibi for the time of the kidnapping, and he spoke and wrote excellent English (the ransom notes had always been written in an illiterate manner). Luckily for the prosecution, Reilly was not competent. In addition, the prosecution, taking no chances, is thought to have paid to have evidence manufactured and witnesses lie. The crowds that jammed the streets of Flemington and the press across the nation seemed convinced of Hauptmann's guilt, and this did his case no good.

One witness that they did not have to pay was Charles Lindbergh, who attended every day of the six-week trial and steadfastly maintained in his testimony that it was Hauptmann's voice that he had heard cry "Hey, Doc!" the night the money changed hands. Anne Lindbergh attended the trial only twice, once when she

*Bruno Hauptmann (right) with
his lawyer, Edward J. Reilly*

testified and once when her mother did; she resolutely stayed away the other days. Her major concerns for those times when she did appear was not to break down or to disappoint Charles. She accomplished this by staring at a blue patch of sky outside the courtroom window and not looking at Hauptmann. The second appearance was the more difficult of the two, she said, because she was "freer to feel." She later wrote in her diary: "How incredible that my baby had any connection with this!"

Hauptmann was found guilty and sentenced to death. Anne wrote in her diary: "The trial is over. We must start our life again, try to build it securely—C. and Jon and I."

The only bright spots during this time were in the personal achievements of Charles and Anne, who were again—temporarily—living at Next Day Hill. Harold Nicolson, a British writer working on a biography of Dwight Morrow, was also living there temporarily, and encouraged Anne in her writing. Anne soon after published her first book, *North to the Orient*, an account of her trip there with Charles in 1931. The book was well received, and for Anne, who had always wanted to be a writer, this was the culmination of a dream. Charles, meanwhile, was working on the perfusion pump with Alexis Carrel. The darkest time was the death of Anne's sister Elisabeth, whose rheumatic fever some years before had caused permanent heart damage and made her susceptible to the pneumonia that killed her. Anne had been very close to Elisabeth, and it was a tremendous blow.

∼

Meanwhile, Anne and Charles were anxious to find a house of their own. They visited Minnesota and considered moving into Charles's childhood home, an idea that appealed more to Charles than to Anne, who struggled valiantly to try to "see it with his eyes." Harry Guggenheim offered them land on Long Island, but in clearing the land the workmen mistakenly burned a number of older trees on the estate, and the Lindberghs never felt the same about it after that. They considered Maine, near the Morrows' summer home, but decided against it when another family moved onto land too close to the location they were considering. Photographers continued to harass the family and were particularly interested in getting pictures of Jon, which enraged Charles.

Finally, Harold Nicolson suggested that they think about settling in England, at least for a while. At that time, England was a quieter, more peaceful, and more secure country than the United States, and the idea appealed to the Lindberghs.

They sailed there on December 22, 1935, and the press was not notified until they were at sea. Numerous editorials expressed disgust that their hero had virtually been run out of his own country. An editorial in the *New York Herald Tribune* said:

The departure of Colonel and Mrs. Lindbergh for England, to find a tolerable home there in a safer and more civilized land than ours had shown itself to be, is its own commentary upon the American social scene. Nations have exiled their heroes; they have broken them with meanness. But when has a nation made life unbearable to one of its most distinguished men through a sheer inability to protect him from its criminals and lunatics and the vast vulgarity of its sensationalists, publicity-seekers, petty politicians and yellow newspapers? It seems as incredible as it is shocking. Yet everyone knows that this is exactly what has happened. . . .

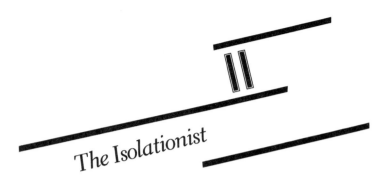

The Isolationist

Harold Nicolson and his wife, the writer Vita Sackville-West, lived near Sissinghurst, Kent, in southeastern England. Their home was an old manor in the Tudor style, but they also owned a large cottage near their home called Long Barn, which Anne lovingly called "an old rambling house fitting the side of a hill." The Lindberghs rented it at $200 a month. Nicolson asked the townspeople of Weald, the closest village, to please leave the Lindberghs alone, and they did so. Anne was able to shop and take walks with Jon without anyone bothering her, and Charles could go into London without hordes of people following. There was one flare-up of publicity, even in the British newspapers, when Bruno Hauptmann was finally executed on April 3, 1936, but by and large the English gave the Lindberghs a wide berth.

This is not to say that they were totally ignored. London society was intrigued by them, and the Lindberghs accepted many invitations to social events. They even had tea with the new king, Edward VIII, and were included in the first banquet given by him since he had succeeded to the throne. The banquet was also notable for being the first occasion that Mrs. Wallis Simpson, whose romance with the king would later cause him to abdicate, was formally present at a royal social function. Charles was unaware of all of this and puzzled that the prime minister, Stanley Baldwin, beside whom he was seated at dinner, seemed uninterested in Charles's ideas on aviation in Britain. He could not know that Baldwin's only thought that evening was of how he could separate Mrs. Simpson and Edward, and that he could concentrate on nothing else. Anne had better luck with the king, who told Nicolson later that although Anne began by being rather shy, "with my well known charm I put her at her ease and liked her very much."

About this time, Lindbergh received a letter from Major Truman Smith, U.S. military attaché, who was in charge of army and air intelligence in Berlin, Germany. Smith was aware that the new National Socialist regime in Germany was building the most powerful air force in Europe, the *Luftwaffe*. Lacking technical knowledge of aviation or aeronautics, he felt that Lindbergh could perform a great service for the American military by making a tour of German aviation centers. He confirmed that the German *Luftwaffe* chief, Hermann Göring, would be glad to have Lindbergh visit and then invited both Charles and Anne to come at their convenience. About two months later, after delivery of a new plane that Lindbergh had asked to be built to his specifications, Charles and Anne took off for Germany.

Germany was hosting the Olympic Games in 1936, and as the eyes of the world were focused on the National

Socialist regime, those in power were mounting a huge public relations campaign. Their plans included entertaining various celebrities from Europe and the United States and an attempt on their part to show only the good side of Nazi Germany. Besides attending the first day of the Olympic Games with Göring, Lindbergh was also the guest of honor at a luncheon given by the Air Club in Berlin, attended a reception given by the mayor of Berlin, had tea with former Crown Prince Wilhelm, and attended a luncheon given by Göring at his official residence. He also visited several aircraft factories and came away with a greatly inflated idea of German air power, thanks to Göring's presenting a vastly exaggerated view of it. Lindbergh was also greatly impressed by the whitewashed view of National Socialism that he received. The German people had seemed more congenial than the British, yet more respectful than the Americans, and the press was not as uncontrolled as it was in the United States. Further, morals seemed to be high. Lindbergh did not see concentration camps or prisons, and had not spoken with any opponents of the Reich. He left feeling good about Germany's future and anxious regarding other countries' defenses against it.

Why was Charles Lindbergh so impressed by all of this? During the early days of his fame, he had been exposed to some of the worst aspects of the American character—excessive prying, excessive adulation, women throwing themselves at him, obscene letters. The behavior of the press during his child's disappearance and death, and during Hauptmann's trial, had only added to his disgust. He was beginning to think that Western democracies were physically and morally decadent.

The question also has to be raised concerning Lindbergh's supposed anti-Semitism, or dislike of Jews.

Hermann Göring (center) with
Charles and Anne in Berlin

There is almost no question that Lindbergh, like many people of his day, considered Jews "different" and, surrounded as he had been by the narrow social set of the Morrows, was inclined to think of Jews as people he wouldn't necessarily seek out socially. However, there is no evidence that Lindbergh was aware of the horrors being perpetrated on Jews in Germany at that time. At the end of World War II, in fact, when he visited concentration camps and saw what had been done, he was appalled. Moreover, he did number some Jews among his friends, including Harry Guggenheim.

When the Lindberghs returned to England, Lindbergh discussed with Harold Nicolson his views on what he had just seen, and Nicolson wrote in his diary: "[Lindbergh] has obviously been much impressed by Nazi Germany. He admires their energy, virility, spirit, organization, architecture, planning, and physique. He considers that they possess the most powerful air force in the world with which they could do terrible damage to any other country. . . . He admits that they are a great menace but denies that they are a menace to us. He contends that the future will see a complete separation between Fascism and Communism, and he believes that if Great Britain supports the decadent French and the Red Russians against Germany, there will be an end to European civilization."

Lindbergh stressed to Nicolson that although he was happy to see Germany growing stronger, because he believed that a strong Germany was important to the overall welfare of Europe, he also believed that this strength should be matched by the British and felt that Britain was falling behind in aviation, as indeed it was. Since World War I, Britain had been in the grip of an intensive pacifist feeling, probably as a result of having an entire generation of young men wiped out. Also, Britain's great political minds—with the exception of Winston Churchill—had been unenthusiastic about building up the military. Lindbergh asked Nicolson to help him get in to see someone in political power, and shortly thereafter he was granted an interview with Sir Thomas Inskip, minister of defense, during which he managed to thoroughly frighten the minister with his prophesies of Germany's rise to power.

Despite the fact that Anne Lindbergh became pregnant about this time, she kept flying with Lindbergh and, in fact, accompanied her husband on a three-month trip to India and the Middle East late in her pregnancy. Their new son, Land, was born on May 12, 1937, the evening of the day that George VI was crowned (his brother had abdicated to marry Mrs. Simpson). That fall, the Lindberghs made a second trip to Germany. Again, the Nazis showed him only the best in their aviation program and falsified their production records so that Lindbergh had a greatly exaggerated view of German strength. For example, Lindbergh estimated that Germany was building between 500 and 800 planes a month, but later records showed that production was under 300 a month. In 1938, the *Luftwaffe* was in no condition to fight the combined forces of Western Europe and the Soviet Union, but Göring believed that if he could trick these nations into believing in Germany's strength, he would never have to fight. In a book published around this time, *Command of the Air*, Giulio Douchet maintained that in the future wars would be won by the biggest bomber force. Lindbergh and most of the leaders of Western Europe were convinced by this book, and

Lindbergh now felt that his primary duty was to ensure that Britain and France stay out of any conflict, as they would surely be wiped out by the "stronger" German force.

Lindbergh shared this view with Nancy Astor, an American-born member of Parliament, who arranged meetings for Lindbergh with the ministers of defense and war, the Fabians (a pacifist group), Joseph P. Kennedy, who was serving as the American ambassador to London, and the American ambassador to Paris. Later, he also spoke to the French minister for air. His dire warnings even reached the ear of the British prime minister, Neville Chamberlain. Lindbergh was even more discouraged after visiting the Soviet Union and Czechoslovakia later that year and seeing their air forces, which did not impress him.

Lindbergh arrived back in London to learn that Hitler was planning to seize the Sudetenland from Czechoslovakia. By treaty, if Czechoslovakia were attacked, the Soviet Union and France, and therefore Britain, were supposed to help defend it. Lindbergh was terrified and wrote a long letter to Joseph Kennedy reiterating his belief in Germany's military might and urging Britain and France to appease Hitler. Kennedy saw to it that before Chamberlain left to meet with Hitler on this issue, he had seen a summary of Lindbergh's letter. Greatly disturbed by Lindbergh's predictions, Chamberlain convinced the French prime minister that they should accede to Hitler's demands. The Munich

Neville Chamberlain (left) shakes hands with Adolf Hitler as the British prime minister arrives in Germany for a meeting.

Pact, signed on September 29, 1938, sacrificed Czechoslovakia to Hitler to keep the peace. Although Lindbergh's
pleas were not the only factor in persuading Chamberlain,
his was perhaps the strongest voice. Shortly after this,
Lindbergh made his third trip to Germany, where he was
decorated by the German government, ostensibly for his
aviation record but no doubt due to their wish to continue
their association with him.

Meanwhile, Lindbergh was beginning to become
irritated with the English people. In contrast to the
qualities of competence, moral purity, and efficiency he
thought he had found in the German people, he found
the English incompetent, inefficient, and decadent. So
in the summer of 1938 the Lindberghs moved to Illiec,
an island off the Brittany coast that had been bought for
them by Dr. and Mrs. Alexis Carrel, who owned a
nearby island, St. Gildas. It was a tiny island, with room
only for four buildings, but the Lindberghs loved its
beauty and the privacy it afforded them. Anne was able to
write in peace, and Charles was able to continue his
scientific experiments with Dr. Carrel. Ironically, the
Lindberghs considered buying a winter home in Berlin,
as Illiec was plagued by winter storms, but they had a
difficult time finding one. The German government
offered to have one built for them, but just then
anti-Jewish riots broke out in Germany. Anne and Alexis
Carrel convinced Lindbergh that Berlin was not where
his family should settle, and they stayed in Paris for the
winter.

Lindbergh did visit Berlin twice more that year and
became involved in a deal to have the French buy
airplane engines from the Germans. No one but Lindbergh really believed that the deal would come off, but
German officials strung him along as long as possible.

In March 1939, Hitler entered Czechoslovakia, and the Munich Pact was dead. Lindbergh felt that Hitler's next move might be against Poland, a move he partially sympathized with because he felt that Hitler was the one leader who could successfully defend Europe against the Soviet threat. However, he knew that should Hitler invade Poland, Britain and France might move in to defend it. He was concerned that the United States might then become involved and decided to return to the United States to try and prevent this. He sailed home in April 1939 and met with the National Advisory Committee, then with President Franklin D. Roosevelt. This would be their first and only meeting, and it left both men with slightly uneasy feelings. Although Roosevelt was not at that time convinced of the necessity to involve America in the conflict, he was much more pro-Allies than was Lindbergh. Moreover, as the complete politician himself, Roosevelt found it hard to believe that Lindbergh's motives were not at least somewhat politically motivated. As a result of this and other meetings, Lindbergh decided that he should stay in America and do what he could to keep the United States out of the war. Anne and the children came over later that month and shared a moment of victory a few weeks later as they watched a Pan American clipper leave with the first load of airmail for Europe, following the route that Anne and Charles had first taken.

Shortly after Anne and the children were comfortably settled in the house that they had rented at Lloyd Neck, Long Island, Lindbergh headed to Washington and began talking with a number of governmental officials, including Vice President John Nance Garner, about the situation in Europe. At this time, some 70 percent of the American people were in favor of neutrality, according to a Gallup poll, and most politicians reflected this feeling. The fact that England and France did nothing when Poland was invaded in September of 1939 reinforced the beliefs of most Americans that this was one conflict they should avoid. After the Polish defeat, Roosevelt made a radio speech in which he promised to keep America neutral and warned Americans to beware of pro-Allies propaganda.

However, Lindbergh still didn't trust the president's motives. Despite his current neutral position, Roosevelt was still clearly pro-Allies and very anxious for them to win, even if he was not prepared at the moment to give military aid. He saw Hitler as a threat to free people everywhere, not just to Western Europe, but believed the dictator could be stopped. Lindbergh's feelings toward Germany were more positive, but overriding everything else were his feelings that it could not be beaten. He felt there was still a need to do everything possible to keep America out of the war. He decided to go on radio himself. The president got wind of this and decided the time had come to get Lindbergh on his side. Through several intermediaries, including Truman Smith, who was now back in Washington, he offered Lindbergh a new cabinet post, secretary of the air. Unfortunately, it was presented to Lindbergh right before he was due to make his first radio speech, and Lindbergh didn't even respond to the president. Although this attempt by Roosevelt could be seen as a bribe, it was also a chance to increase the prestige of flying, strengthen the Air Corps, and enhance Lindbergh's influence with the administration. In retrospect, Lindbergh should have accepted. When he gave no answer of any kind, any chance for cooperation with the administration ended.

In the meantime, Lindbergh began a series of articles and radio talks, all urging Americans to keep out of the war. In this, he had the total support of Anne, which did not endear either of them to the Morrow family. Betty Morrow was staunchly pro-Allies, and Next Day Hill was alive with committees and volunteers who felt the same way. Anne's younger sister Constance, who was married to Aubrey Morgan, was in an even more embarrassing position. Her Welsh husband was assistant chief of the British Information Services in New York, a group that Lindbergh asserted was trying to involve the United States in the war. The situation was not improved when the Lindbergh's lease at Lloyd Neck ran out in October, and the Lindberghs moved back to Next Day Hill. As stories of Nazi atrocities began to surface, a number of their friends also began to avoid them. From England, Harold Nicolson wrote a long article in which he said that Lindbergh's political stance and feelings about Germany stemmed from a revulsion toward democracy caused by the events surrounding the murder of his child.

As Hitler continued his relentless onslaught in Scandinavia, Holland, Belgium, and France, more and more Americans began to feel that Hitler was a threat to the United States as well. Franklin Roosevelt now felt comfortable to run for president in 1940 on a platform that promised help to the Allies, and he was overwhelmingly reelected. Lindbergh was discouraged by the president's popularity but comforted by the fact that there were still a number of isolationist groups. He joined the largest, best known, and most respected: the America First Committee.

Lindbergh speaks at an America First committee rally.

This committee numbered many wealthy and influential persons among its 800,000 members. Its chairman was also the chairman of Sears, Roebuck, and other prominent members included the vice-president of the Central Republic Bank of Chicago; a former national commander of the American Legion; air ace Eddie Rickenbacker; writer Kathleen Norris; film star Lillian Gish; and Alice Roosevelt Longworth, daughter of Theodore Roosevelt and cousin of Franklin. In the fall of 1940, their primary fight was against the Lend-Lease Bill, an act proposed by Roosevelt that would give Britain both armaments and supplies and postpone payment for them. Despite America First's opposition and an emotional speech by Lindbergh to Congress, the bill was passed overwhelmingly. Lindbergh continued to speak throughout the winter and spring of 1941, however, and finally, in a press conference, Roosevelt alluded to him as being a Copperhead, or traitor. In reaction to this, Lindbergh made the disastrous decision to resign his Army Air Corps commission, a move that seemed to many Americans to justify the president's accusation.

It was a difficult time for the Lindberghs. Anne had had another baby in the fall of 1940, a little girl named after herself, but this happy event failed to ease the tensions in the Morrow household. In the summer of 1941, the Lindberghs rented another house on the North Shore of Long Island in order to get away. Both the Lindberghs and their friends the Truman Smiths were under government surveillance at this time, and most of their other friends had abandoned them. Despite this, Lindbergh continued to speak, addressing large audiences all over the country and a huge crowd of 20,000 in Madison Square Garden. The administration, believing that it had to stop Lindbergh at any cost, began making references to the decoration that the Germans had bestowed on him. Unwisely, Lindbergh began to defend himself against the implied charges of collaboration; this only made matters worse. Two months later, he made an even more disastrous mistake. In a speech he was giving in Des Moines, Iowa, he referred to the Jewish influence in the country, which he believed was the leading cause of pro-Allies sentiment, and there was an ugly backlash reaction. His defenders were quick to point out that he had criticized Jewish influence, not the Jews, but most people didn't see the difference. A number of people resigned from the committee, and he was crucified in the press. Despite a warm reception at a second Madison Square Garden appearance in October, his influence was beginning to wane.

Ultimately, it did not matter, because on December 7, 1941, the Japanese bombed Pearl Harbor, and America was in the war.

12
The War Years

Now that we are at war I want to contribute as best I can to my country's war effort. It is vital for us to carry on this war as intelligently, as constructively, and as successfully as we can, and I want to do my part.

Lindbergh wrote these words in his diary on December 12, 1941, five days after Pearl Harbor, and he meant them. In order to fulfill what he believed to be his duty to his country, his first instinct was to write to President Roosevelt, but he hesitated to do so because "the President has the reputation, even among his friends, for being a vindictive man. If I wrote to him at this time, he would probably make what use he could of my offer from a standpoint of politics and publicity and assign me to some position where I would be completely ineffective and out of the way." Instead, he wrote to General Arnold of the Army Air Corps. When the general did not respond to the letter for several weeks, Lindbergh called his office and was told to make an appointment with the secretary of war, Henry L. Stimson. What he did not know was that Secretary of the Interior Harold Ickes had not forgotten Lindbergh's America First activities and was determined to keep him out—or at least on the sidelines—of the war. Ickes wrote the following letter to Roosevelt (quoted in Mosley, p. 308):

December 30, 1941. My dear Mr. President: I notice that Lindbergh has just offered his services to the Army Air Corps. I believe that, taking the long view, it is of the utmost importance that the offer should not be accepted.

An analysis of Lindbergh's speeches and articles—I have a complete indexed collection of them—has convinced me that he is a ruthless and conscious fascist. . . . His actions have been coldly calculated with a view to obtaining ultimate power for himself—what he calls "new leadership." Hence it is important for him to have a military service record.

It is a striking historical fact that every single dictator and half-dictator in postwar Europe had a military service record. Mussolini was a war veteran. Mustapha Kemal Pasha was a war veteran. Horthy was a war veteran. Hitler was a war veteran. The same is true of the fascists. Leaders who never achieved power but came close to doing so: Colonel de la Rocque in France, Starhemberg in Austria, for example.

To accept Lindbergh's offer would be to grant this loyal friend of Hitler's a precious opportunity on a golden platter. It would, in my opinion, be a tragic disservice to American democracy to give one of its bitterest and most ruthless enemies a chance to gain a military record. I ardently hope that this convinced fascist will not be given the opportunity to wear the uniform of the United States.

He should be buried in merciful oblivion. Sincerely yours, Harold L. Ickes

Roosevelt replied (Mosley, p. 309):

Dear Harold: What you say about Lindbergh and the potential danger of the man I agree with wholeheartedly. As ever, FDR.

Therefore, when Lindbergh met with Secretary of War Stimson, Stimson had already been given orders not to offer Lindbergh a commission. He gave the following account of their meeting (Mosley, pp. 301–11):

When he came in yesterday, he told me that he was thinking of going into the business of airplane manufacture, but that he did not wish to do so until he had offered his Government to help it in the present emergency in any way that he could. I thanked him and told him of my own position on this matter, as announced the other day at my Press conference, namely that I would welcome any information or suggestions that might come to me from him or any other American which would help us in our work in the Department.

I told him that to that end I would arrange for his meeting with [General] Arnold and [Assistant Secretary] Lovett, to work out details with us. But I also told him that I would not be frank if I did not make it clear to him now that from my reading of his speeches, it was clear to me that he took a very different view of our friends and enemies in the present war from not only that of ourselves but from that of the great majority of our countrymen, and that he evidently lacked faith in the righteousness of our cause.

I told him that we were going to have a very difficult and hard war on our hands, and that I should be personally unwilling to place in command of our troops as a commissioned officer any man who had such a lack of faith in our cause, as he had shown in his speeches.

I then sent for Lovett and turned him over to Lovett to talk over his suggestions in detail. Though evidently rather set back by my frankness, he thanked me cordially for seeing him and for giving him this opportunity for even limited service.

Lindbergh's humiliation was not yet over. When he offered his aviation expertise to Pan American, United Aircraft, and Curtiss-Wright for the duration of the war, he was thanked politely but firmly turned down. The Roosevelt administration was determined to punish him for his antiwar activities, and it looked for a few months as though they would succeed, until another famous person heard about Lindbergh's problems and decided to help.

~

Henry Ford and Charles Lindbergh had much in common. Both were mechanical geniuses, both were non-drinkers and nonsmokers, both were hardworking, both were admirers of many of Nazi Germany's attributes, both loathed Franklin D. Roosevelt, and both were against the war with Germany. Henry Ford, however, had been put in charge of making B-24 bombers at a plant near Detroit called Willow Run, and he was determined to have the best technical help possible. He felt that Charles Lindbergh was the best. So Lindbergh went to work for Ford as a technical consultant at the Willow Run plant for $666 per month, a sum exactly equal to what he would have made had he been in the Army Air

Corps, and Anne and the three children joined him there in the spring of 1942.

The B-24 bombers were the first to be built in the assembly-line format that had been the source of Henry Ford's fame. Because of his flying experience, Lindbergh was able to suggest a number of improvements in the bomber itself, as well as in the process of manufacturing and assembling it; he also flight-tested it. Partially because of his contributions, the Willow Run plant was able to mass-produce more planes than anyone had previously.

In August 1942 Anne Lindbergh gave birth to another son, who was called Scott. The Lindberghs were living in a small house in Bloomfield Hills, a well-to-do suburb of Detroit. Between too many children and too little space, Anne sometimes felt overwhelmed, but Charles bought a trailer which was kept on the grounds, and Anne used it as a place to write. Living in Detroit also gave Lindbergh frequent opportunities to see his mother, who lived nearby and was getting frail. She, in turn, loved having Lindbergh and the grandchildren close at hand.

Lindbergh was also hired during this period as a high-altitude test pilot for the Republic Aircraft Corporation. He was forty years old—elderly for this kind of work—so before he began he went to the Mayo Clinic in Rochester, Minnesota, and worked with the Aero Medical Unit in a series of tests in its high-altitude chamber. He learned how to recognize the signs of anoxia, or lack of oxygen, and therefore was able to take corrective action in high altitudes before tragedy could occur. This training was once put to good use at 41,000 feet (12,300 m), when a faulty gauge registered that it had oxygen when it didn't. He described the incident in his later book *Of Flight and Life* (pp. 3–7):

Forty thousand feet and still climbing, I am running an ignition breakdown test on the engine of a Thunderbolt [single-place monoplane] fighter. Research in the higher air is a relief from my wartime routine of conferences, production lines, and bomber shakedown flights. At 41,000 feet, I level off, set the trim tabs, and adjust the turbo. I must hold five minutes of level flight while plane and engine settle down to normal readings.

All goes well until, test run and readings logged, I start to descend. Then, at 36,000 feet: something happens to clarity of air, to pulse of life, perception of eye. I grow aware of that vagueness of mind and emptiness of breath which warn a pilot of serious lack of oxygen. I force myself to alertness—I must think or die! The idea lashes brain and body like the blow of a whip. Mask leaking? I shove it up with my left hand—no, tight against my face. Out of oxygen? No. (A glance at the gauge shows 50 pounds.) Then something must be wrong with the oxygen system. I know from altitude-chamber experience that I have about 15 seconds of consciousness left at this altitude—neither time nor clearness of mind to check hoses and connections. Life demands oxygen and the only sure supply lies 4 miles beneath me.

I shove the stick forward. The earth slants upward and the dive begins . . . 35,000 feet . . . 34,000 my cockpit roars through the air . . . the lungs, empty—I'm blacking out—losing sight. . . . I push the nose down farther . . . faster . . . 33,000 . . . 30,000 . . . the dials become meaningless . . . down . . . down. . . . I am dimly aware of a great shriek, as though a steam whistle were blowing near my ears. . . . Compressibility dive? I'm not thinking about compressibility . . . it's oxygen I need. . . . I'm blind. . . . I can't see the needles . . . there are no more seconds left—it's a razor edge—a race between decreasing consciousness and increasing density of air . . . 17,000 . . . 16,000 . . . 15,000 . . . a white needle moves over white figures . . . it's the altimeter—I can see—I'm reading its dial again—I'm aware of the cockpit, the plane, the earth and sky—I've already begun to pull out of the dive—the stick is free; the nose rising; the seat pressing against me. The air in my lungs has substance. Perception floods through nerve and tissue. How clear the sky is above me, how wonderful the earth below.

Lindbergh's experiences at the Mayo Clinic also resulted in improvements in high-altitude equipment, work that would later save many lives.

Despite these accomplishments, Lindbergh was still unhappy that he was not participating more actively in the war, so he jumped at the chance to go out to the South Pacific and see how the new bombers were performing. He had to go as a civilian, and his appearance was kept under wraps for fear of action by the administration and also for fear of what the Japanese would do if they knew that Charles Lindbergh was in the sky above them. Despite this, he flew in fifty combat missions and for 179 combat hours. He shot down one plane by himself and participated in the shooting down of several others. At forty-two, he was extremely old for a fighter pilot, but he showed extreme competence and coolness under fire and was able to teach the younger men how to fly in a way that would conserve gas—crucial during a time when gasoline was at a premium—and how to use their planes to maximum advantage. He was with them for four months and would have been there longer had there not been publicity about him almost being shot down. Lindbergh described this incident in his diary (p. 892):

An enemy fight is above us, at six o'clock, diving on us. I give the alarm. MacDonald and Miller turn back. The

Zero is swinging around onto Smith's tail. I turn back. Smith is heading for a cloud. The Zero shifts his attack to me. I have turned too soon. He is too far above for me to climb into him. I would be in a stall by the time I reached his altitude, and that is fatal with a Zero.

I bank right to give MacDonald and Miller a better chance to cut in toward me. I push the r.p.m. full forward and the throttles to the fire wall. The propellers surge up past 3,000. The manifold reaches sixty inches. But he has altitude advantage. He is closing on my tail—almost within gun range now.

I am not high enough to dive. It is useless to try to outturn a Zero. I must depend on speed and armor plate and the other members of my flight. I nose down a little and keep on turning to avoid giving him a no-deflection shot. He must have his guns on me now—in perfect position on my tail.

I hunch down in front of the armor plate and wait for the bullets to hit. I think of Anne—of the children. My body is braced and tense. There is an eternity of time. The world was never clearer. But there is no sputtering of an engine, no fragments flying off a wing, no shattering of glass on the instrument board in front of me.

The Zero is climbing away. MacDonald has forced him off with a long deflection shot. Smith gets in a second burst as he flashes past. Miller comes in on one wing and starts the Zero smoking. We last see it zooming skyward toward the nearest cloud.

Lindbergh still had his humanity, however, as one can see from this entry in his journal (p. 821):

Out to the coast line—four Corsairs abreast, racing over the water—I am the closest one to land. The trees pass, a streak of green; the beach a band of yellow on my left. Is it a post a mile ahead in the water, or a man standing? It moves toward shore. It is a man.

All Japanese or unfriendly natives on New Ireland— everything is a target—no restrictions—shoot whatever you see. At 1,000 yards my .50-calibers are deadly. I know just where they strike. I cannot miss.

Now he is out of the water, but he does not run. The beach is wide. He cannot make the cover of the trees. He is centered in my sight. My finger tightens on the trigger. A touch, and he will crumple on the coral sand.

But he disdains to run. He strides across the beach. Each step carries dignity and courage in its timing. He is not an ordinary man. The shot is too easy. His bearing, his stride, his dignity—there is something in them that has formed a bond between us. His life is worth more than the pressure of a trigger. I do not want to see him crumple on the beach. I release the trigger.

I ease back on the stick. He reaches the tree line, merges with the streak of green on my left. I am glad I have not killed him. I would never have forgotten him writhing on the beach. I will always remember his figure striding over the sand, the fearless dignity of his steps. I had his life balanced on a muscle's twitch. I gave it back to him, and thank God that I did so. I shall never know who he was—Jap or native. But I realize that the life of this unknown stranger—probably an enemy—is worth a thousand times more to me than his death. I should never quite have forgiven myself if I had shot him—naked, courageous, defenseless, yet so unmistakably man.

In September 1944, Lindbergh returned to the United States, and he and Anne found a house in Darien, Connecticut. In the spring of 1945, President Roosevelt died while the war was finally coming to a successful end. United Aircraft, for whom Lindbergh was working as a technical consultant, asked him to go to Germany to see what advances German scientists had made in aeronautics. Lindbergh left in May 1945 and arrived in Paris six days after the Germans had surrendered. He looked for two of his old friends, but Michel Detroyat, an old flying friend, was missing, and Mme. Carrel, who was brokenhearted over her husband's recent death and also the false accusations that he had collaborated with the Germans, had just left for the United States. So Lindbergh went on to Germany.

There he found that there was intense competition between the Americans, the British, the French, and the Russians over the German scientists, a competition that the Germans used to their best advantage. Lindbergh wrote long reports on the state of German aviation for United Aircraft and suggested often that the German scientists be brought over to the United States as soon as possible. But his diaries during the month he was away dealt less with scientific technology than with his indignation at the way he believed the German people were being treated. He felt that the Allies should be kinder to the conquered people and was particularly concerned with the children, to whom he was constantly dispensing food from his ration kit.

While he was there, he had the chance to go to Berchtesgaden, Hitler's mountain retreat. He described the trip in his journal (p. 949):

We made our way over the debris on the floor of the room said to be Hitler's office to the great oblong gap which was one once filled with a plate-glass window. It framed almost perfectly a high Alpine range—sharp gray crags, white fields of snow, sawtooth peaks against a blue sky, sunlight on the boulders, a storm forming up the valley. It was one of the most beautiful mountain locations I have ever seen. As one steps closer to the window, the eyes travel down the mountainside with the ledge—snow fields and bare rocks to deep green forests to steeply sloping fields to the well-kept fields and groups of farm buildings in the valley. To the left the valley disappears amid Alpine mountain peaks, a breeding ground for storms like the one now forming. To the right, through a gap in the mountains, one sees level Bavarian plains extending to the horizon.

It was in this setting, I realize, that the man Hitler, now the myth Hitler, contemplated and laid his plans— the man who in a few years threw the human world into the greatest convulsion it has ever known and from which it will be recuperating for generations. A few weeks ago he was here where I am standing, looking through that window realizing the collapse of his dreams, still struggling desperately against overwhelming odds. This scene, this valley, these mountains entered into the contemplation, the plans which brought such disaster to the world. Hitler, a man who controlled such power, who might have turned it to human good, who used it to such resulting evil: the best youth of his country overrun by the forces he feared most, the forces of Bolshevism, the armies of Soviet Russia; much of his country, like his own room and quarters, rubble—flame-blackened ruins.

While Lindbergh was in Germany, he was taken to see Camp Dora, one of the German concentration camps. His journal captured his horror at what he saw (pp. 995–96):

Here was a place where men and life and death had reached the lowest form of degradation. How could any reward in national progress even faintly justify the establishment and operation of such a place? When the value of life and the dignity of death are removed, what is left for man?. . . .

We are standing in front of what was once a large oblong pit, probably eight feet long and six feet wide and, one might guess, six feet deep. It is filled to overflowing with ashes from the furnaces—small chips of human bones—nothing else.

A trail of these ashes runs over the side of the filled-up pit where we are standing. They were dumped in carelessly, as we would dump the ashes from coal into a pit at home. And the pit was dug as a man would dig a pit for coal ashes if he cared nothing for the appearance of the grounds around his home—not very far from the furnaces and where the ground appeared easy to dig. Nearby were two oblong mounds, which may have marked other pits. The boy picks up a knee joint which had not been left in the furnace long enough and holds it out to us.

Of course, I knew these things were going on; but it is one thing to have the intellectual knowledge, even to look at photographs someone else has taken, and quite another to stand on the scene yourself, seeing, hearing, feeling with your own senses.

Interestingly, Lindbergh compared the German extermination of the Jews to the violent treatment he had occasionally witnessed of the Japanese by Americans in the Pacific, which tended to be isolated incidents and not systematic annihilation. It was as though he could not really believe that the Germans in whom he had believed so strongly in the late thirties could have been capable of the mass destruction that he saw with his own eyes.

He tried to visit Britain before he came home but was advised that his behavior before the war made it inadvisable for him to be there at that time. He returned to Connecticut, his family, and the postwar world.

~

13
Picking Up the Pieces

After living in Connecticut in a rented house for a short time, the Lindberghs decided that they liked the area and bought a home near Scott's Cove, Darien, on the Long Island Sound. Anne gave birth to her sixth and last child in the fall of 1945, a daughter they called Reeve, and the family settled down to what Charles and Anne hoped would be a quiet family life. Charles still didn't think the family was big enough—he had wanted twelve children—but he settled for his five. The house was furnished simply for a family with the Lindberghs' financial resources, but there was a fine piano and several good pieces of art. Neither Anne nor Charles ever cared much about furniture, and a simple house made it easier to raise children. The children attended the local public schools, and neighborhood children were in and out of the house constantly.

It was the closest to real privacy that the Lindberghs had ever enjoyed, and the younger children were able to grow up without being affected too much by their father's fame. Lindbergh had very definite ideas about how to raise children; he was determined that they should be as unspoiled and independent as possible. They earned their allowances by doing tasks around the house and yard and would receive a substantial bonus if they were able to identify quotations at the dinner table. From an early age they were taught to be fearless, and all grew up to be quite independent. They also had complete confidence in their father. One day, when Lindbergh and his youngest daughter, Reeve, were out flying in a small plane, the engine died in midair. Reeve, quite naturally, asked her father if they were going to crash. Her father said "no" quite firmly, and Reeve immediately relaxed. Luckily, Lindbergh was able to glide the plane into a field, and both were unhurt.

With five children around the house, Lindbergh found it necessary to work in a trailer, which he kept parked in his backyard. The nature of his work was such that, unlike most fathers, he would often be around for days or weeks at a time. However, a new project might suddenly send him off to exotic places—often without his family even knowing where he was. "Actually, he wasn't away as much as it seemed," one of the Lindbergh children was once quoted as saying. "It's just that we never knew where he was or when he was coming back."

One of the first jobs Lindbergh took after the war was as a civilian adviser to the armed forces, at a salary of $1 a year. He was consulted on rocketry and various other space matters and the national defense. He also acted as an adviser to the U.S. Air Force in Europe in 1949. At this time Soviet forces were trying to prevent supplies from getting into West Berlin in order to force the city to join the Communist bloc, and the Air Force was trying to airlift supplies into the city for its cold and hungry inhabitants. Lindbergh, who was violently opposed to the Soviets, as always, was thrilled to be able to advise the Air Force on how to react should the Soviet forces try to prevent the airlift. He himself participated in the airlift and seemed disappointed when the Soviets didn't try to stop him. In his pep talks to the forces stationed in the area, he always emphasized the importance of their mission in light of the Cold War.

Charles was also appointed to the Air Force Scientific Advisory Board. In this capacity he attended conferences on space projects and also spent time on the testing grounds of the Southwest, watching the experiments that were taking place at the time. There he would often work with some of the German scientists that he had known in Germany in the thirties, who had been brought over to participate in the U.S. space program. The current focus of the space program was manned spaceflight and how to safeguard the astronauts who would eventually go into space. From his experiments at the Mayo Clinic during the war, Lindbergh had an extensive knowledge of how people physically react in rarefied air, and he was able to pass on this knowledge. Years later, astronauts such as Neil Armstrong would be amazed at his knowledge in this area: "He talked to us about things like air stresses, acceleration tolerance, the so-called Oxygen Paradox as if the guy had spent hours in air pressure chambers himself," said Armstrong. "Turned out he had, too. He knew more about some of the problems than the doctors did."

Lindbergh also supported the Pentagon buildup of weaponry. The Cold War was at its height, and Lindbergh believed that the only defenses against the forces of communism were bigger and stronger deterrents. "Our objective is the survival of Western civilization," he wrote in an article for the *Saturday Evening Post*, "and our policy must be dynamic. There is no longer such a thing as adequate defense. As long as a dangerous enemy exists, our security will lie in our indestructible power to destroy."

Lindbergh also tested most of the Air Forces' new jets, although he was by now in his fifties, and also went on B-52 bomber patrols over the Arctic. He regained his job as a consultant to Pan Am, and much of his work at the time involved traveling the various routes the company had around the world. He was still interested in the expansion of air service. He worked on the development of the Boeing 707, the largest plane up to that time, and was involved in the early work on supersonic transport.

Despite all of his achievements, however, Lindbergh had not lost his power to incite controversy. During the McCarthy hearings in Washington, his failure to speak out against witch-hunts of alleged Communists was severely criticized. Although no fan of McCarthy, he seemed to feel that the spread of communism was so rampant that every other danger paled beside it. His Cold War stance and interest in weapons buildup brought criticism from those who felt that such an attitude could only lead the country—and indeed the world—into a frightening and dangerous weapons race. He also wrote a book called *Of Flight and Life*, which not only expounded his belief in aggressive weaponry but also implied that unrestricted immigration would spell the end of America, a belief that sounded very racist. This received wide criticism. Interestingly, the book also showed hints of a plea by Lindbergh for a return to a nontechnological world and a simpler, more basic life.

This was a theme that was beginning to occur more

and more frequently in his writings and speeches. In 1949, when he was presented with the Wright Brothers Memorial Trophy at the Washington Aero Club, he accepted the trophy for "significant public service of enduring evaluation to aviation and the United States" and made a plea for not allowing science to separate man from his spiritual and moral qualities:

In honoring the Wright brothers, it is customary and proper to recognize their contribution to scientific progress. But I believe it is equally important to emphasize the qualities in their pioneering life and the character in man that such a life produced. The Wright brothers balanced success with modesty, science with simplicity. At Kitty Hawk their intellects and senses worked in mutual support. They represented man in balance, and from that balance came wings to lift a world.

In 1952 Lindbergh approached his friend, the writer J. P. Marquand, with a manuscript. For years Marquand had wanted Lindbergh to write about the 1927 flight. Marquand loved the script and immediately submitted it to the Book-of-the-Month Club. Shortly thereafter, the *Saturday Evening Post* paid $100,000 for the serial rights. It was published in 1953 as *The Spirit of St. Louis* and shortly thereafter won the Pulitzer Prize for biography. Its initial failure as a film was a disappointment for Lindbergh, but it did gain him a new friendship, with actor James Stewart. The two men shared several common interests, including flying and conservative political views. By this time, they shared another interest—the Air Force Reserve. President Eisenhower restored Lindbergh's commission in the armed forces in April 1954, and Lindbergh was sworn in as a brigadier general in the

James Stewart plays Lindbergh in the movie
The Spirit of St. Louis. He and the pilot become
good friends after the movie was released.

Air Force Reserve. Despite the controversy that still surrounded him, for Lindbergh it was a recognition from Washington that his loyalty to his country could not be questioned.

Anne Lindbergh was not feeling as optimistic. Both Lindberghs had lost their mothers in the mid-fifties, and Anne took it particularly hard. Charles seemed to be home only rarely, the older children were married or away at school, and the younger children seemed especially demanding when Charles was not around to keep order. She had been having less luck with her writing than Charles had been having and had produced a book of poetry in the early fifties that had been savaged by the press. She was wondering what to do next.

What she did do was to go to a small southern island—by herself—for a short time to get away from it all. She wrote, walked, watched birds, and left behind "the butcher, the baker, and the candlestick maker," as she herself expressed it. For a while her sister Constance joined her, but it was primarily a solitary experience. From this experience, she wrote the book *Gift from the Sea*, which became one of the best-selling books of the fifties. In it, she advocated the premise that all women—indeed, all people—needed greater simplicity and solitude in their lives, and she discussed how such qualities could be brought into the extremely fragmented life of twentieth-century America. The book had enormous impact on women everywhere, and it would ultimately be the work for which Anne Lindbergh would be best remembered.

When she returned to her normal life, she determined that the lessons of the book would not be lost on herself; one of the ways in which she insured this a few years later was with Argonauta, a home on Maui,

Hawaii, built to be a place of quiet refuge for herself and Charles. A Pan Am associate and friend had offered them four acres on this beautiful island, and Charles and Anne had enthusiastically accepted. Their home had no electricity, which helped them to simplify their lives in ways that Anne had discussed in *Gift from the Sea*. They usually spent about six to eight weeks a year there and planned to spend more as the years progressed and they retired. Nature surrounded them there, which pleased both of them, but for Charles it was beginning to become more than a pleasure. He didn't know it yet, but nature was about to lead him to perhaps his most important achievement.

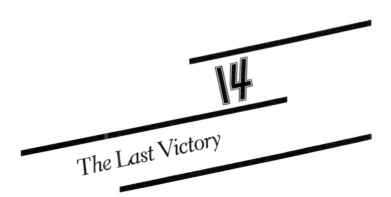

14

The Last Victory

Lying under an acacia tree, with sounds of dawn around me, I realized more clearly, in fact, what man should never overlook: that the construction of an airplane, for instance, is simple when compared with the evolutionary achievement of a bird; that airplanes depend upon advanced civilization; and that where civilization is most advanced, few birds exist.

I realized that if I had to choose, I would rather have birds than airplanes. I began to question the definition I had assigned to progress.

This incident, quoted in Mosley's biography of Lindbergh, page 365, occurred in 1964 on a trip to Kenya. Lindbergh had been in New York, meeting with representatives from Curtiss-Wright, General Electric, and Pratt and Whitney. They were discussing the Concorde, the supersonic plane developed by England and France, and debating what kind of supersonic plane America should build. Lindbergh suddenly felt a need to get away. He left the meeting, went to the airport, and was in Kenya three days later. The next morning, on awakening, he began to question his overall approach to living, an approach that had placed science and technology ahead of nature. But as Lindbergh looked around him, it seemed to him that humankind had not always gained in the process. He described his disgust in *Autobiography of Values* (p. 40):

Within a fraction of my lifetime, I saw New York parking space disappear, the waters of Long Island Sound become polluted, and the coasts of Maine and Florida packed to the shoreline with houses and motels. The distant howl of a superhighway and the thunder of jet aircraft in the sky broke into the tranquility of my New England home. Rampant pressures of improved technology and increasing population were rapidly destroying what I considered freedom.

As a result of these feelings, Lindbergh began to focus on conservation issues. Upon his return to the United States, he became a member of the World Wildlife Fund and a year later was on its board. He also joined the National Union for the Conservation of Nature and through this organization became interested in the plight of blue and humpbacked whales. These whales were being harpooned by the thousands and were in danger of extinction. Lindbergh went on a Peruvian whaling expedition in the South Pacific to see what was happening and was horrified by the killing he saw. He was even more horrified when he discovered that the whale-killing operation was owned by an American company.

He immediately contacted the company's president, convinced him of the righteousness of his cause, and was ultimately able to arrange for a Peruvian ban on harpooning.

Because of his reputation and influence, Lindbergh was able to contact important people and cut through much red tape. Other organizations, such as the Nature Conservancy and the Oceanic Foundation, wanted him to help them, also. Soon he was busy saving the polar bear, the one-horned rhinoceros, and various species of marine life.

During this period Anne Lindbergh bought a chalet in Switzerland, and while staying there Lindbergh became a member of the Geneva committee of the World Wildlife Fund. Through this committee he met Tom Harrisson, an English conservationist. Harrisson convinced Lindbergh to go with him to the Philippines and rescue the tamarau, a small buffalo native only to that region. It had almost been wiped out by Filipino hunters, and Harrisson believed that only a big public relations campaign would help to stop this slaughter. Lindbergh agreed and, despite his normal avoidance of the press, decided to work with them to achieve his end. He took a *New York Times* reporter with him on the trip to the Philippines and into the jungle and used every opportunity for a story or a picture. In Manila he talked President Ferdinand Marcos into issuing a protective decree. A short time later, he also convinced Marcos to issue a decree protecting the monkey-eating eagle, a species that then numbered only sixty. In both of these cases, Lindbergh's trips into the jungle were under very primitive conditions, and despite his being in his sixties, he slept anywhere, ate whatever was available, and never seemed to tire. He also developed a warm relationship

Lindbergh poses for a picture with
Philippines president Ferdinand Marcos
(in front of painting), his wife (right),
and their children.

with the Filipino people and did a good job of convincing them of the importance of saving the tamarau and the eagles.

The only bleak spot during this period was in late 1966, when Harold (now Sir Harold) Nicolson published his diaries and letters for the years 1930 to 1939. In them, he spoke of the period when the Lindberghs were living at Long Barn and making trips to Germany. When the book came out, it stirred up some of the old controversy that the Lindberghs thought they had successfully put behind them. Lindbergh claimed that there were several inaccuracies in Nicolson's reporting and that several of his remarks had been taken out of context and were therefore easily misinterpreted. He immediately wrote to Nicolson, but Sir Harold, who was quite elderly by this time, was unable to respond to the letter. His son Nigel, who had edited the diaries and letters, was sympathetic but refused to retract any of the statements made in them. Lindbergh felt that some kind of response had to be made, so in 1970 he published his own diaries, written from 1938 to 1945, under the title *The Wartime Journals of Charles A. Lindbergh.* In them, it seemed as though he were trying to justify his behavior and his beliefs, both before and during the war, and many people who had forgotten how angry they had been with him became angry all over again. Yet, as controversial as the book was, it did not sell well nor was it well received by the critics.

Anne Lindbergh had better luck with her own diaries and letters, which she began to publish in 1971. The first, *Bring Me a Unicorn,* dealt with her college years and her romance with Charles up until the time they became engaged. *Hour of Gold, Hour of Lead* dealt with their early marriage, their trip to the Orient, and the birth and death of their first baby. *Locked Doors and Open Rooms* dealt with the period of Hauptmann's trial, her sister's death, more travel, and finally the Lindberghs' decision to emigrate to England. Later she was to publish two more books: *The Flower and the Nettle*, which dealt with their years in Europe, and *War Within and Without*, which dealt with their lives during the isolationist period and World War II. Her diaries were better received than Charles's writings were, possibly because she included introductions and notes that added illumination to her diaries and letters. When she had been wrong, she admitted it; this made her readers more sympathetic.

Charles decided to leave the world of letters and return to his latest cause—conservation. His last great effort came not with saving an animal but with saving a group of people, the Tasadays.

The Tasadays had been discovered in the jungles of Mindanao Island in the Philippines by a native hunter in the 1960s. They were a primitive tribe that had remained virtually unchanged since the Stone Age. These very small people lived without clothing in caves; swung through trees; ate roots, insects, dead animals, and fish; and possessed only the crudest stone tools. They had no history and no religion, but also no wars, murders, or enemies. Their world was about to change, however. Mindanao was an extremely violent and lawless island, and once it was revealed that the Tasadays existed, their peaceful life—and their safety—was in jeopardy. The president of Panamin (the Private Association for National Minorities) appealed to Lindbergh for help, and Lindbergh immediately flew out to Mindanao to investigate. He found the tiny Tasadays totally appealing as a people—friendly, childlike, not even possessing a word for bad. Their way of life seemed to reinforce Lindbergh's contention that civilization often did people more harm than good.

NBC wanted to do a news segment on the tribe, and the National Geographic Society wanted to do a documentary. Lindbergh talked Panaman into letting them do what they wanted but for hundreds of thousands of dollars. The money was used to support Panamin's programs, and the resulting publicity caused the Philippine government to set aside over 46,000 acres of land as a Tasaday reserve. Once more, the Lindbergh name had been used in a good cause.

Unfortunately, in the 1980s, charges were made that the Tasadays were not as primitive as Lindbergh had believed—that they were, in fact, part of a hoax perpetrated on Lindbergh and the media by Panamin. These charges have never been conclusively proven, and the anthropological community remains divided on the issue. The truth may never be known, because modern influences among many of the tribes in the Philippines may have affected the Tasadays in the fifteen years since Lindbergh's visits. Nevertheless, Lindbergh's efforts in focusing worldwide attention on the tribe cannot be discounted.

Just over a year after his work with the Tasadays, Lindbergh came down with what seemed at first to be a rash and a fever that persisted for months. He was unable to continue with several conservation projects and was forced to resign from the board of Pan Am. It was not until the summer of 1974, however, that he learned what was really wrong with him—lymphatic cancer. He immediately said that he wished to die in the home that he and Anne had built in Maui, and he was flown there in August 1974. As he left the hospital for the airport, doctors followed him to the door, protesting that he should not leave. One doctor cried out, "But you're abandoning science!" Lindbergh quietly but humorously replied, "No. Science has abandoned me." Lindbergh died in Maui a week later, on August 25, 1974, and was buried in the local churchyard.

~

Charles Lindbergh never entirely regained the prestige and honor that he had had before his opposition to World War II, and there were many people who never forgave him for his views. Certainly, his knowledge of world affairs at the time was naïve at best, and it is perhaps unfortunate that his fame allowed him to be in a position where his views could be heard by so many. His honesty—or perhaps his obstinacy—also prevented him from ever really changing his views about what the United States should have done in the thirties and forties and what would have ultimately been the best solution to Hitler as well as to the Communist threat. An unworldly, even somewhat narrow, individual, he was not able to appreciate the vast social changes that occurred after World War II, and his conservationist stance was in many ways a harkening back to a simpler way of life that the world had lost forever and that he greatly missed.

No one can dispute, however, that he was an immensely brave man whose accomplishments went far beyond his feat of crossing the Atlantic. Without very much formal education, he obtained a thorough knowledge of science and mechanics that brought changes and advances not only to aviation but also to other technologies, including medical research. Moreover, his work in the field of conservation was a pioneering effort that did much to stimulate interest in the field and remains one of his greatest achievements. A number of species still exist because of his efforts. Possessing in his youth an almost totally scientific approach to life, he became more and more interested in its human side as he grew older. In the book that he was working on at the time of his death, later published as *Autobiography of Values*, he stated (p. 402):

The growing knowledge of science does not refute man's intuition of the mystical. Whether outwardly or inwardly, whether in space or in time, the farther we penetrate the unknown, the vaster and more marvelous it becomes. . . .

I am form and I am formless. I am life and I am matter, mortal and immortal. I am one and many— myself and humanity in flux. I extend a multiplicity of ways in experience and space. . . .

After my death, the molecules of my being will return to the earth and the sky. They came from the stars. I am of the stars.

Bibliography

Allen, Frederick Lewis. *Only Yesterday*. New York: Harper & Row, 1931.

Beamish, Richard J. *The Story of Lindbergh, The Lone Eagle*. New York: The International Press, 1927.

Collier, Peter, and David Horowitz. *The Fords: An American Epic*. New York: Summit Books, 1987.

Davis, Kenneth S. *The Hero: Charles A. Lindbergh and the American Dream*. Garden City, N. Y.: Doubleday and Company, Inc., 1959.

Gill, Brendan. *Lindbergh Alone*. New York: Harcourt Brace Jovanovich, Inc., 1977.

Kennedy, Ludovic. *The Airman and the Carpenter: The Lindbergh Kidnapping and the Framing of Richard Hauptmann*. New York: Viking Penguin, Inc., 1985.

Lindbergh, Anne Morrow. *Bring Me a Unicorn*. New York: Harcourt Brace Jovanovich, Inc., 1971.

———. *Gift from the Sea*. New York: Pantheon, 1955.

———. *Hour of Gold, Hour of Lead*. New York: Harcourt Brace Jovanovich, Inc., 1973.

———. *Listen! the Wind*. New York: Harcourt, Brace, and Company, 1938.

————. *Locked Rooms and Open Doors.* New York: Harcourt Brace Jovanovich, Inc., 1974.

————. *North to the Orient.* New York: Harcourt, Brace and Company, 1938.

————. *The Flower and the Nettle.* New York: Harcourt Brace Jovanovich, Inc., 1976.

————. *War Within and Without.* New York: Harcourt Brace Jovanovich, Inc. 1980.

Lindbergh, Charles A. *Autobiography of Values.* New York: Harcourt Brace Jovanovich, Inc., 1976.

————. *Boyhood on the Upper Mississippi: A Reminiscent Letter.* St. Paul: Minnesota Historical Society, 1972.

————. *Of Flight and Life.* New York: Charles Scribner's Sons, 1948.

————. *The Spirit of St. Louis.* New York: Charles Scribner's Sons, 1953.

————. *The Wartime Journals of Charles A. Lindbergh.* New York: Harcourt Brace Jovanovich, Inc., 1970.

————. *We.* New York: G.P. Putnam's Sons, 1927.

Manchester, William. *The Last Lion: Winston Spencer Churchill; Alone: 1932–1940.* Boston: Little, Brown and Company, 1988.

Mosley, Leonard. *Lindbergh: A Biography.* Garden City, N.Y.: Doubleday and Co., Inc., 1976.

Nicolson, Nigel, ed. *Harold Nicolson: Diaries and Letters, 1930-1939.* London: William Collins Sons and Company, 1966.

Putnam, George Palmer. *Soaring Wings.* New York: Harcourt, Brace, and Company, 1939.

Ross, Walter S. *The Last Hero: Charles A. Lindbergh.* New York: Harper & Row, Publishers, Inc., 1964.

Waller, George. *Kidnap: The Story of the Lindbergh Case.* New York: The Dial Press, 1961.

Whipple, Sidney B. *The Lindbergh Crime.* New York: Blue Ribbon Books, 1935.

The author is also indebted to the *New York Times* for its excellent reportage during the major events of Lindbergh's life, particularly during the periods of May and June 1927, March through August 1932, and January and February 1935.

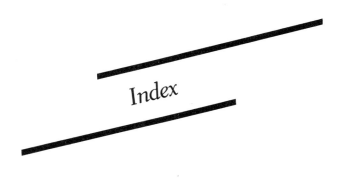

Index